EVERYDAY Literacy
Science

GRADE
K

Download Home–School Activities in Spanish

The Home–School Connection at the end of each weekly lesson in the book is also available in Spanish on our website.

How to Download:

1. Go to www.evan-moor.com/resources.

2. Enter your e-mail address and the resource code for this product—EMC5025.

3. You will receive an e-mail with a link to the down-loadable letters, as well as an attachment with instructions.

Writing: Barbara Allman
Content Editing: Guadalupe Lopez
Lisa Vitarisi Mathews
Andrea Weiss
Copy Editing: Cathy Harber
Art Direction: Cheryl Puckett
Kathy Kopp
Cover Design: Cheryl Puckett
Illustrator: Ann Iosa
Design/Production: Carolina Caird

EMC 5025

Evan-Moor
EDUCATIONAL PUBLISHERS
Helping Children Learn since 1979

Visit
teaching-standards.com
to view a correlation
of this book.
This is a free service.

*Correlated to State and
Common Core State Standards*

Congratulations on your purchase of some of the finest teaching materials in the world.

Contents

What's Inside

In this book, you will find **20 weekly lessons**. Each weekly lesson includes:

3 Teacher Pages

Use these pages to guide you through the week.

A script to follow that introduces the science concept

A short story to read aloud to students

Daily discussion questions about the story or science concept, plus a script to guide students through the activities

A hands-on activity that reinforces the weekly concept

Samples of students' expected responses

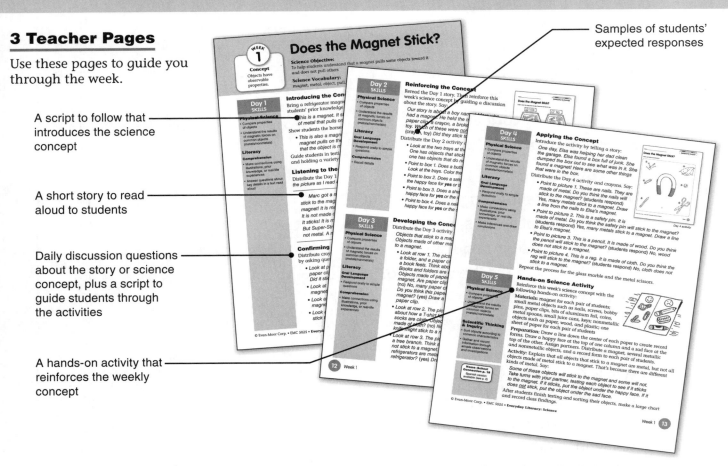

4 Student Activity Pages

Reproduce each page for students to complete during the daily lesson.

1 Home–School Connection Page

At the end of each week, give students the **Home–School Connection** page (in English or Spanish) to take home and share with their parents.

To access the Spanish version of the page, go to www.evan-moor.com/resources. Enter your e-mail address and the resource code EMC5025.

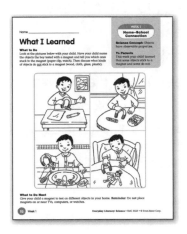

How to Use This Book

Follow these easy steps to conduct the lessons:

Day 1

Reproduce and distribute the *Day 1 Student Page* to each student.

Use the scripted *Day 1 Teacher Page* to:

1. Introduce the weekly concept.

2. Read the story aloud as students listen and look at the picture.

3. Guide students through the activity.

Days 2, 3, and 4

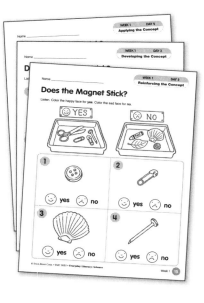

Reproduce and distribute the appropriate day's activity page to each student.

Use the scripted *Teacher Page* to:

1. Review and discuss the Day 1 story.

2. Reinforce, develop, apply, or extend the science concept.

3. Guide students through the activity.

Day 5

Follow the directions to lead the Hands-on Science Activity.

Send home the **Home–School Connection** page for each student to complete with his or her parents.

Home–School Connection

Tips for Success

- Review the *Teacher Page* before you begin the lesson.

- Work with students in small groups at a table in a quiet area of the room.

- Model how to respond to questions by using complete sentences. For example, if a student responds to the question "Where does rain come from?" by answering "clouds," you'd respond, "That's right. Rain comes from the clouds."

- Wait for students to complete each task before giving the next direction.

- Provide visual aids or concrete demonstrations when possible.

Skills Chart

	Science																			
	Physical Science						Life Science					Earth Science								
Week	Observe and describe properties of objects	Compare properties of objects	Understand the results of magnetic forces on common objects (metals/nonmetals)	Understand that water can be a solid, a liquid, or a gas	Understand properties of solids and liquids	Identify tools and simple machines used for a specific purpose	Associate each of the five senses with a part of the body	Understand that our five senses help us learn about the world around us	Understand that plants, animals, and people are living things that have basic needs	Understand that animals, plants, and people are living things that have parts	Understand that people and animals are living things that grow and change	Understand that the sun, moon, and stars are objects in our sky	Explore properties of the moon and the stars	Understand that the Earth is composed of air, land, and water	Distinguish between bodies of water	Understand that rocks have different properties	Understand that the seasons change in a pattern	Understand that there are different kinds of weather	Identify the phases of the water cycle	Understand that land, air, and water affect the weather
1		•	•																	
2	•	•																		
3	•				•															
4	•			•																
5						•														
6																				
7							•	•												
8										•										
9										•										
10											•									
11											•									
12										•										
13										•										
14										•										
15																	•	•		
16												•	•							
17												•	•							
18														•	•					
19														•			•			
20																			•	•

Scientific Thinking and Inquiry					Investigation		Literacy — Oral Language Development							Literacy — Comprehension					Week
Record observations and data with pictures and other symbols	Sort objects according to common characteristics	Experiment with simple machines	Gather and record information through simple observations and investigations	Make inferences and draw conclusions	Understand that the position of objects can be described	Identify and describe objects in a given position	Use descriptive language	Give and follow directions	Name and describe pictured objects	Respond orally to simple questions	Use traditional structures, such as chronological order, to convey information	Use traditional structures, such as cause and effect, to convey information	Use new vocabulary	Recall details	Make connections using illustrations, prior knowledge, or real-life experiences	Answer questions about key details in a text read aloud	Make inferences and draw conclusions	Respond appropriately to verbal commands	
	•		•							•				•	•	•	•		1
	•		•				•		•	•				•	•	•			2
			•	•			•		•	•	•	•		•	•	•			3
			•							•	•	•		•	•	•			4
		•	•						•	•				•	•	•			5
					•	•		•		•			•	•	•	•			6
•			•				•			•				•	•	•	•		7
•			•	•						•		•		•	•	•	•		8
•									•	•			•	•	•	•	•		9
•									•	•	•		•	•	•	•	•		10
	•								•	•	•			•	•	•	•		11
	•								•	•			•	•	•	•	•		12
•										•			•	•	•	•	•		13
									•	•			•	•	•	•		•	14
•									•	•			•		•	•	•		15
			•							•				•	•	•	•		16
•									•	•			•	•	•	•			17
			•							•			•	•	•	•	•		18
	•			•			•		•	•				•	•	•	•		19
			•	•						•		•	•	•	•	•	•		20

Everyday Literacy
Science

Student Progress Record

Name: _____

Write dates and comments in the boxes below the student's proficiency level.

1: Rarely demonstrates   0 – 25 %
2: Occasionally demonstrates   25 – 50 %
3: Usually demonstrates   50 – 75 %
4: Consistently demonstrates   75 – 100 %

Pre-Literacy Concepts	1	2	3	4
Communicates using drawing and tracing				
Tracks print and pictures from top to bottom and left to right				
Understands that pictures and symbols have meaning and that print carries a message				

Oral Language Development

Uses descriptive language				
Names and describes pictured objects				
Responds orally to simple questions				

Comprehension

Recalls details				
Makes connections using illustrations, prior knowledge, or real-life experiences				
Listens to stories being read aloud				
Makes inferences and draws conclusions				

Science

Uses content vocabulary when speaking				
Engages in scientific thinking and inquiry				

Everyday Literacy: Science • EMC 5025 • © Evan-Moor Corp.

Everyday Literacy
Science

Small-Group Record Sheet

Students' Names:

Write dates and comments about students' performance each week.

Week	Title	Comments
1	Does the Magnet Stick?	
2	Shapes, Sizes, and More	
3	Solids and Liquids	
4	Where Did the Water Go?	
5	Wheels Do the Work	
6	Tell Where It Is	
7	My Five Senses	
8	What Plants Need	
9	What Animals Need	
10	From Egg to Frog	
11	I'm Growing!	
12	Animals Have Parts	
13	Trees Have Parts	
14	My Body Has Parts	
15	Four Seasons	
16	The Moon	
17	What Is a Star?	
18	Bodies of Water	
19	Looking for Rocks	
20	The Water Cycle	

Dear Parent or Guardian,

Every week your child will learn a concept that focuses on Physical, Life, or Earth Science. Your child will develop oral language and comprehension skills by listening to stories and engaging in oral, written, and hands-on activities that reinforce science concepts.

At the end of each week, I will send home an activity page for you to complete with your child. The activity page reviews the weekly science concept and has an activity for you and your child to do together.

Sincerely,

Estimado padre o tutor:

Cada semana su niño(a) aprenderá sobre un concepto de ciencias físicas, naturales o de la Tierra. Su niño(a) desarrollará las habilidades de lenguaje oral y de comprensión escuchando cuentos y realizando actividades orales y escritas. Además, participará en actividades prácticas que apoyan los conceptos de ciencias.

Al final de cada semana, le enviaré una hoja de actividades para que la complete en casa con su niño(a). La hoja repasa el concepto científico de la semana, y contiene una actividad que pueden completar usted y su niño(a) juntos.

Atentamente,

Does the Magnet Stick?

Science Objective:
To help students understand that a magnet pulls some objects toward it
and does not pull others

Science Vocabulary:
magnet, metal, object, pull, stick

Day 1 SKILLS

Physical Science
• Compare properties
of objects
• Understand the results
of magnetic forces on
common objects
(metals/nonmetals)

Literacy

Comprehension
• Make connections using
illustrations, prior
knowledge, or real-life
experiences
• Answer questions about
key details in a text read
aloud

Introducing the Concept

Bring a refrigerator magnet and a horseshoe magnet to class. Activate
students' prior knowledge by showing them the refrigerator magnet. Say:

• *This is a magnet. It sticks to a refrigerator. A magnet is a kind
of metal that pulls on certain things.*

Show students the horseshoe magnet and say:

• *This is also a magnet. When we place some things next to it, the
magnet pulls on them. If an object sticks to a magnet, we know
that the object is made of metal.*

Guide students in testing the magnet on different surfaces in the room
and holding a variety of small objects up to it to see what "sticks."

Listening to the Story

Distribute the Day 1 activity page to each student. Say: *Listen and look at
the picture as I read a story about a boy who finds out what sticks to a magnet.*

---

*Marc got a magnet for his birthday. He is excited to see what will
stick to the magnet. First, Marc tries a paper clip. It sticks to the
magnet! It is made of metal. Next, he tries a crayon. It does not stick.
It is not made of metal. Then he tries his big brother's broken watch.
It sticks! It is metal. Last, he tries his favorite toy, Super-Stretch Nick.
But Super-Stretch Nick does not stick. Can you guess why? Nick is
not metal. A magnet cannot pull on him, but Marc can!*

Confirming Understanding

Distribute crayons. Develop the science concept
by asking questions about the story. Say:

• *Look at picture 1. Why did Marc hold the
paper clip to the magnet?* (to see if it sticks)
Did it stick? (yes) *Circle the paper clip.*

• *Look at picture 2. Did the crayon stick to the
magnet?* (no) *Draw an X on the crayon.*

• *Look at picture 3. Did the watch stick to the
magnet?* (yes) *Circle the watch.*

• *Look at picture 4. Did Super-Stretch Nick
stick to the magnet?* (no) *Draw an X on Nick.*

Day 1 picture

Physical Science
- Compare properties of objects
- Understand the results of magnetic forces on common objects (metals/nonmetals)

Literacy

Oral Language Development
- Respond orally to simple questions

Comprehension
- Recall details

Reinforcing the Concept

Reread the Day 1 story. Then reinforce this week's science concept by guiding a discussion about the story. Say:

Our story is about a boy named Marc who had a magnet. He held the magnet next to a paper clip, a crayon, a broken watch, and a toy. Which of these were <u>not</u> made of metal? (crayon, toy) Did they stick to the magnet? (no)

Distribute the Day 2 activity and crayons. Say:

- *Look at the two trays at the top of the page. One has objects that stick to a magnet and one has objects that do not.*
- *Point to box 1. Does a button stick to a magnet? Look at the trays. Color the happy face for* **yes** *or the sad face for* **no***. (no)*
- *Point to box 2. Does a safety pin stick to a magnet? Look at the trays. Color the happy face for* **yes** *or the sad face for* **no***. (yes)*
- *Point to box 3. Does a shell stick to a magnet? Look at the trays. Color the happy face for* **yes** *or the sad face for* **no***. (no)*
- *Point to box 4. Does a nail stick to a magnet? Look at the trays. Color the happy face for* **yes** *or the sad face for* **no***. (yes)*

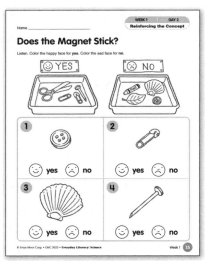

Day 2 activity

Physical Science
- Compare properties of objects
- Understand the results of magnetic forces on common objects (metals/nonmetals)

Literacy

Oral Language Development
- Respond orally to simple questions

Comprehension
- Make connections using illustrations, prior knowledge, or real-life experiences

Developing the Concept

Distribute the Day 3 activity and crayons. Say:

Objects that stick to a magnet are metal. Objects made of other materials don't stick to a magnet.

- *Look at row 1. The pictures show a book, a folder, and a paper clip. Think about how a book feels. Think about how a folder feels. Books and folders are made from paper. Objects made of paper do not stick to a magnet. Are paper clips made of paper? (no) No, many paper clips are made of metal. Do you think this paper clip might stick to a magnet? (yes) Draw a circle around the paper clip.*

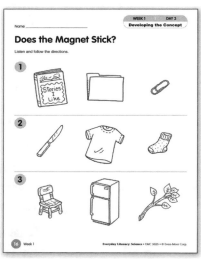

Day 3 activity

- *Look at row 2. The pictures show a knife, a T-shirt, and a sock. Think about how a T-shirt feels. Think about how a sock feels. T-shirts and socks are cloth. Objects made of cloth do not stick to a magnet. Is a knife made of cloth? (no) No, most knives are made of metal. Do you think a knife might stick to a magnet? (yes) Draw a circle around the knife.*
- *Look at row 3. The pictures show a wooden chair, a refrigerator, and a tree branch. Think about how wood feels. Objects made of wood do not stick to a magnet. Are refrigerators made of wood? (no) No, many refrigerators are metal. Do you think a magnet might stick to a refrigerator? (yes) Draw a circle around the refrigerator.*

Day 4
SKILLS

Physical Science
- Compare properties of objects
- Understand the results of magnetic forces on common objects (metals/nonmetals)

Literacy

Oral Language Development
- Respond orally to simple questions

Comprehension
- Make connections using illustrations, prior knowledge, or real-life experiences
- Make inferences and draw conclusions

Applying the Concept

Introduce the activity by telling a story:

One day, Elsa was helping her dad clean the garage. Elsa found a box full of junk. She dumped the box out to see what was in it. She found a magnet! Here are some other things that were in the box.

Distribute the Day 4 activity and crayons. Say:

- *Point to picture 1. These are nails. They are made of metal. Do you think the nails will stick to the magnet?* (students respond) *Yes, many metals stick to a magnet. Draw a line from the nails to Elsa's magnet.*

- *Point to picture 2. This is a safety pin. It is made of metal. Do you think the safety pin will stick to the magnet?* (students respond) *Yes, many metals stick to a magnet. Draw a line to Elsa's magnet.*

- *Point to picture 3. This is a pencil. It is made of wood. Do you think the pencil will stick to the magnet?* (students respond) *No, wood does not stick to a magnet.*

- *Point to picture 4. This is a rag. It is made of cloth. Do you think the rag will stick to the magnet?* (students respond) *No, cloth does not stick to a magnet.*

Repeat the process for the glass marble and the metal scissors.

Day 4 activity

Day 5
SKILLS

Physical Science
- Compare properties of objects
- Understand the results of magnetic forces on common objects (metals/nonmetals)

Scientific Thinking & Inquiry
- Sort objects according to common characteristics
- Gather and record information through simple observations and investigations

Home–School Connection p. 18
Spanish version available (see p. 2)

Hands-on Science Activity

Reinforce this week's science concept with the following hands-on activity:

Materials: magnet for each pair of students; small metal objects such as nails, screws, bobby pins, paper clips, bits of aluminum foil, coins, metal spoons, small juice cans, keys; nonmetallic objects such as paper, wood, and plastic; one sheet of paper for each pair of students

Preparation: Draw a line down the center of each paper to create record forms. Draw a happy face at the top of one column and a sad face at the top of the other. Assign partners. Distribute a magnet, several metallic and nonmetallic objects, and a record form to each pair of students.

Activity: Explain that all objects that stick to a magnet are metal, but not all objects made of metal stick to a magnet. That's because there are different kinds of metal. Say:

Some of these objects will stick to the magnet and some will not. Take turns with your partner, testing each object to see if it sticks to the magnet. If it sticks, put the object under the happy face. If it does <u>not</u> stick, put the object under the sad face.

After students finish testing and sorting their objects, make a large chart and record class findings.

Does the Magnet Stick?

Does the Magnet Stick?

Listen. Color the happy face for **yes**. Color the sad face for **no**.

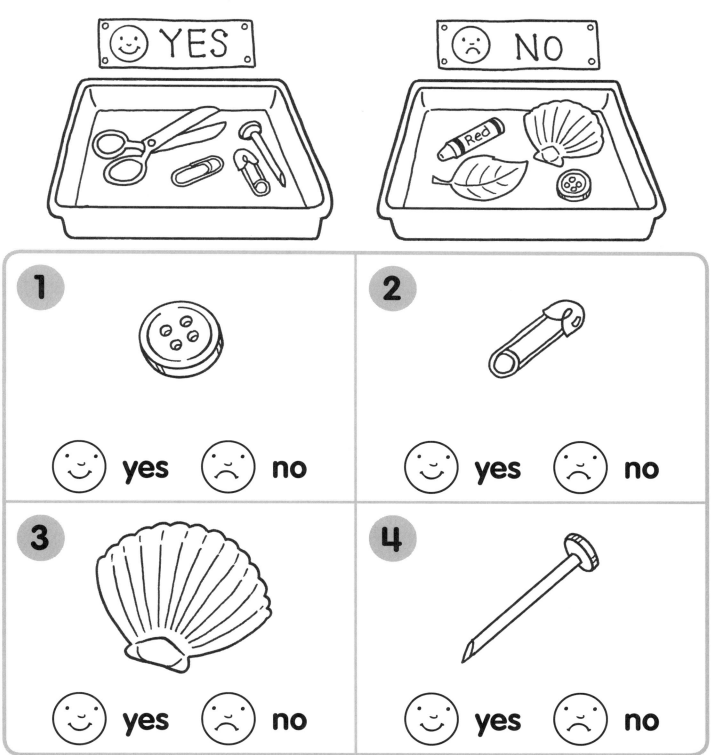

Name _____

Does the Magnet Stick?

Listen and follow the directions.

1

2

3

 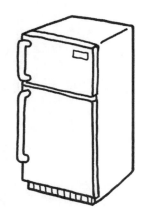 

Name _____

Does the Magnet Stick?

Listen and follow the directions.

1

2

3

4

5

6

Name _____

What I Learned

What to Do

Look at the pictures below with your child. Have your child name the objects the boy tested with a magnet and tell you which ones stuck to the magnet (paper clip, watch). Then discuss what kinds of objects do <u>not</u> stick to a magnet (wood, cloth, glass, plastic).

WEEK 1

Home–School Connection

Science Concept: Objects have observable properties.

To Parents
This week your child learned that some objects stick to a magnet and some do not.

What to Do Next

Give your child a magnet to test on different objects in your home. **Reminder:** Do **not** place magnets on or near TVs, computers, or watches.

Everyday Literacy: Science • EMC 5025 • © Evan-Moor Corp.

Shapes, Sizes, and More

Science Objective:
To engage students in identifying properties of an object, such as its shape, color, size, and texture

Science Vocabulary:
biggest, bumpy, color, orange, red, rough, round, shape, size, smallest, smooth, texture

Objects have different shapes, colors, sizes, and textures.

Day 1
SKILLS

Physical Science
• Observe and describe properties of objects
• Compare properties of objects

Literacy

Oral Language Development
• Use descriptive language
• Name and describe pictured objects
• Respond orally to simple questions

Comprehension
• Make connections using illustrations, prior knowledge, or real-life experiences
• Answer questions about key details in a text read aloud

Introducing the Concept

Hold up or point to a variety of objects around the classroom that have different shapes, colors, sizes, and textures. Say:

*Everything in our world has a **shape**, a **color**, and a **size**. It also feels a certain way when we touch it. It can feel rough or smooth. That's called **texture**.*

• *Point to something you see in the room and tell us what color and shape it is.* (students respond one at a time)

• *Now point to something in the room and tell what you think it feels like. Is it smooth? bumpy? scratchy?* (students respond one at a time)

Listening to the Story

Distribute the Day 1 activity page to each student. Say: *Listen and look at the picture as I read about children who have different fruits.*

My name is Edward and I have an apple. My apple is red, round, and smooth. My friend Emma has a strawberry. Her strawberry is red, heart-shaped, and bumpy. Piper has an orange. It is orange-colored, round, and bumpy. Jordan has a plum. The plum is purple, round, and smooth. We put our fruits side by side to see which one is the biggest and which is the smallest. My red apple is the biggest in size. Emma's strawberry is the smallest. Our fruits have different colors, shapes, and sizes. But one thing about them is the same. They are all good to eat!

Confirming Understanding

Distribute crayons. Reinforce the science concept by asking questions about the story. Ask:

• *Which fruits in the picture have a round shape?* (apple, orange, plum) *Draw a line under the round fruits.*

• *The children told us that some of their fruits felt bumpy. Which fruits felt bumpy?* (strawberry, orange) *Draw a circle around those fruits.*

• *Which fruit in the picture is the biggest?* (apple) *Make an **X** on the apple.*

Day 1 picture

Day 2
SKILLS

Physical Science
- Observe and describe properties of objects
- Compare properties of objects

Literacy

Oral Language Development
- Use descriptive language
- Name and describe pictured objects
- Respond orally to simple questions

Comprehension
- Recall details

Reinforcing the Concept

Reread the Day 1 story. Then reinforce this week's science concept by guiding a discussion about the story. Say:

The children in our story told us about their fruits. Which two fruits did they say felt smooth? (apple, plum)

Distribute the Day 2 activity and crayons. Say:

- *Look at the apples in row 1. Point to the one that is different. How is it different?* (Its size is different; it is smaller.) *Draw a circle around the small apple.*

- *Look at the strawberries in row 2. Point to the one that is different. How is it different?* (Its size is different; It is bigger.) *Draw a circle around the big strawberry.*

- *Look at the fruits in row 3. Point to the one that is different. How is it different?* (Its shape is different; It is not round.) *What kind of fruit is it?* (pear) *Draw a circle around the pear.*

- *Look at the fruits in row 4. Point to the one that is different. How is it different?* (Its texture is different; It looks like it feels bumpy.) *Draw a circle around the orange.*

Day 2 activity

Day 3
SKILLS

Physical Science
- Observe and describe properties of objects
- Compare properties of objects
- Respond orally to simple questions

Literacy

Oral Language Development
- Use descriptive language
- Name and describe pictured objects

Comprehension
- Recall details

Applying the Concept

Distribute the Day 3 activity and crayons. Then introduce the activity by saying:

- *Point to the fruits in box 1. What do you see?* (apple, plum) *Are they the same size?* (no) *Which one is smaller?* (plum) *Color the plum purple.*

- *Point to the fruits in box 2. What do you see?* (apple, banana, pear) *Are the apple, banana, and pear all the same shape?* (no) *Trace around each fruit.*

- *Point to the fruits in box 3. What do you see?* (strawberry, orange) *Did the children in the story say these fruits felt smooth or bumpy?* (bumpy) *Color the strawberry red. Color the orange orange.*

- *Point to the fruits in box 4. What do you see?* (lemon, apple, pineapple) *Which of these looks like it feels smooth?* (apple) *Color the apple red.*

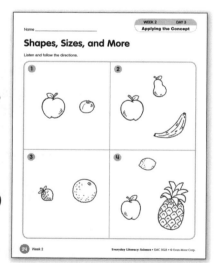

Day 3 activity

Everyday Literacy: Science • EMC 5025 • © Evan-Moor Corp.

Applying the Concept

Distribute the Day 4 activity and crayons. Then introduce the activity by saying:

The food we eat has a size, a color, and a texture. For example, scrambled eggs are soft and yellow, and carrots are crunchy and orange. Look at the picture. The boy in the picture is named Jamal. Jamal is eating lunch. I'll tell you about the food he's eating.

- *Jamal is eating a peanut butter and jelly sandwich for lunch. Have you ever eaten a peanut butter and jelly sandwich?* (students respond) *Was it hard or soft?* (soft) *What shape is Jamal's sandwich?* (square) *Trace around the big sandwich at the bottom of the page.*

- *Jamal is eating tortilla chips for lunch. Have you ever eaten tortilla chips?* (students respond) *Were they hard and crunchy, or soft?* (hard and crunchy) *What shape are Jamal's tortilla chips?* (triangle) *Trace around the big tortilla chip at the bottom of the page.*

- *Jamal is eating a peach for lunch. Have you ever eaten a peach?* (students respond) *How did it feel when you touched it?* (fuzzy, smooth, soft) *What shape is Jamal's peach?* (round) *Trace around the big peach at the bottom of the page.*

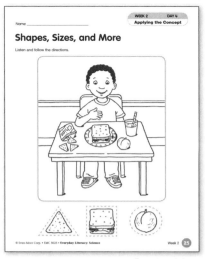

Day 4 activity

Hands-on Science Activity

Reinforce this week's science concept with the following hands-on activity:

Materials: crackers of various shapes (square, round, triangular, etc.), sizes, colors, and textures

Preparation: Assign partners. Give each pair of students a similar group of crackers.

Activity: Introduce the activity by saying:

Objects can be different in many ways. For example, these crackers have different shapes, sizes, colors, and textures.

Then describe a cracker, using as many attributes as possible (small, white, round, smooth). Have partners work together to find the cracker you describe.

Extend the Lesson: Give negative clues and have students identify the cracker you are describing. For example, you might say:

It is not big (students remove big crackers); *it is not square* (students remove square crackers); *it is not brown* (students remove brown crackers); *it is not bumpy* (students remove bumpy ones).

Name _____

Shapes, Sizes, and More

Everyday Literacy: Science • EMC 5025 • © Evan-Moor Corp.

Shapes, Sizes, and More

Listen and follow the directions. Circle the one that is different.

1

2

3

4

Name _____

Shapes, Sizes, and More

Listen and follow the directions.

Everyday Literacy: Science • EMC 5025 • © Evan-Moor Corp.

Name _____

Shapes, Sizes, and More

Listen and follow the directions.

Name _____

What I Learned

What to Do
Have your child look at the picture below, name the fruits, and describe their shapes, sizes, and textures. Then ask your child to color the apple and strawberry red, the plum purple, and the orange orange.

Science Concept: Objects have different shapes, colors, sizes, and textures.

To Parents
This week your child learned to identify properties of an object, such as shape, color, size, and texture.

What to Do Next
Provide three or four different fruits and have your child sort them into groups by size, shape, color, or texture. Then ask your child to tell you about each group he or she makes, for example, *These are all smooth; These are all red; These are all round.*

Solids and Liquids

Science Objective:
To help students understand solid and liquid states of matter by observing water and ice

Science Vocabulary:
flow, freeze, ice, liquid, melt, pour, solid, water

Day 1 SKILLS

Physical Science
- Observe and describe properties of objects
- Understand properties of solids and liquids

Literacy

Oral Language
- Name and describe pictured objects
- Respond orally to simple questions

Comprehension
- Make connections using illustrations, prior knowledge, or real-life experiences
- Answer questions about key details in a text read aloud

Introducing the Concept

Before the lesson, freeze a paper cup full of water. During the lesson, display the frozen cup beside a cup filled with liquid water and an empty bowl. Show students what is in each cup and say: *Both of these cups have water in them.*

- *In one cup, the water is a **liquid**. I can pour it.* Pour the water into the bowl. Say: *A liquid flows from one place to another.*

- *What do you see in the other cup?* (ice) *Ice is also water, but it is a **solid**. It is hard. When liquid water gets very, very cold, it becomes solid ice. A solid is something that has a shape. It does <u>not</u> flow. What do you think happens when ice gets warm again?* (it melts; changes to liquid)

Listening to the Story

Distribute the Day 1 activity page to each student. Say: *Listen and look at the picture as I read a story about how water changes.*

Marissa decided to make ice cubes. First, she poured water into a tray. She was careful not to spill the water. Water spills because it is a liquid. A liquid flows, or moves. Then Marissa put the tray into the freezer. Later, the water had turned to ice. It was still water, but it was a solid. A solid holds its shape and does not flow. Marissa put some ice cubes in a cup and went outside. Soon, the cubes were gone and the cup was filled with water. Marissa knew what had happened: the ice had melted! The solid water had changed back to a liquid.

Confirming Understanding

Distribute crayons. Reinforce the science concept by asking questions about the story. Ask:

- *Does water flow?* (yes) *Look at the first picture. Where do you see water flowing?* (pouring from the pitcher) *Draw a circle around the flowing water.*

- *Can water change into a solid?* (yes) *Look at the second picture. Where do you see solid water?* (ice cubes in tray and glass) *Draw a circle around the ice cubes.*

- *Look at the last picture. What happens to ice when it is left out in the warm air?* (it melts) *Draw a circle around the melted ice.*

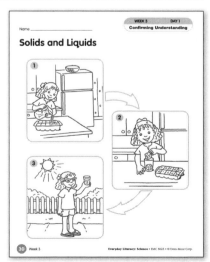

Day 1 picture

Physical Science
• Observe and describe properties of objects
• Understand properties of solids and liquids

Literacy

Oral Language Development
• Use descriptive language
• Respond orally to simple questions

Comprehension
• Recall details
• Make connections using illustrations, prior knowledge, or real-life experiences

Reinforcing the Concept

Reread the Day 1 story. Then reinforce this week's science concept by guiding a discussion about the story. Say:

We learned that water can change from a liquid to a solid and back to a liquid. What do we call solid water? (ice)

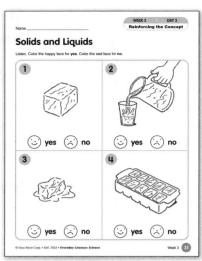

Day 2 activity

Distribute the Day 2 activity and crayons. Say:

• *Point to box 1. What do you see?* (ice cube) *Is it a liquid? Color the happy face for* ***yes*** *or the sad face for* ***no****.* (no) *Is it still water?* (yes)

• *Point to box 2. What do you see?* (water pitcher and glass) *Does water flow when it's a liquid? Color the happy face for* ***yes*** *or the sad face for* ***no****.* (yes)

• *Point to box 3. What do you see?* (melting ice cube) *Can water change from a solid to a liquid? Color the happy face for* ***yes*** *or the sad face for* ***no****.* (yes) *How?* (It can melt, changing from ice to water.)

• *Point to box 4. What do you see?* (ice cube tray) *Can water change from a liquid to a solid? Color the happy face for* ***yes*** *or the sad face for* ***no****.* (yes) *How?* (It can freeze into ice.)

Physical Science
• Observe and describe properties of objects
• Understand properties of solids and liquids

Literacy

Oral Language Development
• Respond orally to simple questions
• Use traditional structures, such as chronological order, to convey information

Comprehension
• Recall details
• Make connections using illustrations, prior knowledge, or real-life experiences

Applying the Concept

Distribute the Day 3 activity and crayons. Ask:

Have you ever tried to eat a frozen treat that started to drip? (students respond) *Why do you think your treat started to drip?* (It was melting.)

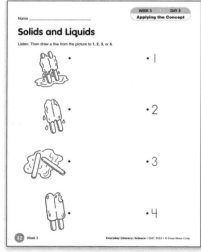

Day 3 activity

• *Look at the pictures. Which picture shows how the frozen treat looked when you first started eating it?* (solid pop with bite missing) *Draw a line from that picture to the number 1.*

• *Which picture shows what happened next?* (beginning to melt) *Draw a line from that picture to the number 2.*

• *Which picture shows what happened third?* (half of frozen treat is gone, melting into a puddle) *Draw a line from that picture to the number 3.*

• *Which picture shows what happened last?* (frozen treat completely melted) *Draw a line from that picture to the number 4.*

Physical Science
- Observe and describe properties of objects
- Understand properties of solids and liquids

Literacy

Oral Language Development
- Respond orally to simple questions
- Use traditional structures, such as cause and effect, to convey information

Comprehension
- Make connections using illustrations, prior knowledge, or real-life experiences

Developing the Concept

Introduce the activity by reviewing:

An ice cube is water in a solid form. A solid keeps its shape. It doesn't flow like a liquid. But water can change when ice melts.

- *Think of something else you have seen that melted. What was it? Where was it?* (students respond)

Distribute the Day 4 activity and crayons. Say:

- *Look at picture 1. Is the ice cube solid?* (yes) *What will happen if it melts?* (It will turn into liquid water.) *Which picture shows what happened when the ice cube melted?* (glass with water in it) *Draw a line to it.*

- *Look at picture 2. What do you see?* (ice cream) *Do you think ice cream can melt into a liquid?* (yes) *Yes, ice cream can melt. Draw a line to the picture that shows melted ice cream.*

- *Look at picture 3. What do you see?* (chocolate bar) *Do you think solid chocolate can melt into a liquid?* (yes) *Yes, chocolate can melt. Draw a line to the picture that shows melted chocolate.*

- *Look at picture 4. What do you see?* (solid stick of butter) *Can solid butter melt into a liquid?* (yes) *Yes, butter can melt. Draw a line to the picture that shows melted butter on toast.*

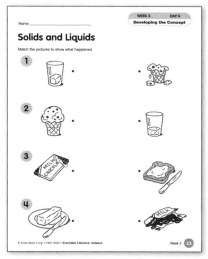

Day 4 activity

Physical Science
- Observe and describe properties of objects
- Understand properties of solids and liquids

Scientific Thinking & Inquiry
- Gather and record information through simple observations and investigations
- Make inferences and draw conclusions

Home–School Connection p. 34
Spanish version available (see p. 2)

Hands-on Science Activity

Reinforce this week's science concept with the following hands-on activity:

Materials: three or more ice cubes and paper plates

Preparation: Use a marker to write a number on each plate. Place each ice cube on a numbered plate.

Activity: Ask students what will happen to the ice cubes. (They will melt.) Then ask:

- *Do you think the ice cubes will all melt at the same time?* (students respond)

- *How can we make the ice cubes melt at different times?* (Place them in different places around the room and outdoors.)

Ask students to suggest places to set the ice cube plates (for example, in a sunny window, in a shady place, by an open window, outdoors, near the air conditioner or heater, and so on). Then observe which one melts first, second, and third. Record the results as a class.

Name _____

Solids and Liquids

Everyday Literacy: Science • EMC 5025 • © Evan-Moor Corp.

Name _____

Solids and Liquids

Listen. Color the happy face for **yes**. Color the sad face for **no**.

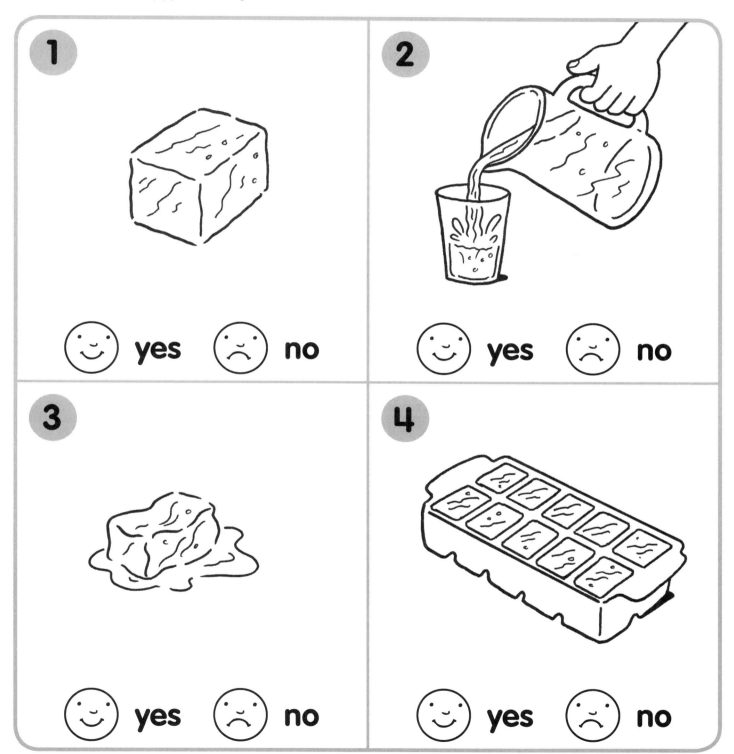

1

☺ yes ☹ no

2

☺ yes ☹ no

3

☺ yes ☹ no

4

☺ yes ☹ no

Name _____

Solids and Liquids

Listen. Then draw a line from the picture to **1**, **2**, **3**, or **4**.

 •   • |

 •   •2

 •   •3

 •   •4

Everyday Literacy: Science • EMC 5025 • © Evan-Moor Corp.

Name _____

Solids and Liquids

Match the pictures to show what happened.

1  •   •

2  •   •

3  •   •

4  •   •

Name _____

What I Learned

What to Do

Ask your child to explain what it means when something is liquid (it flows; it takes the shape of its container) and when something is solid (it keeps its shape). Then look at the pictures with your child and have him or her point out the liquid and solid water.

What to Do Next

Help your child conduct a simple experiment to observe ice melting. Take out two plates. Place an ice cube on each plate. Sprinkle one ice cube with salt. Observe which ice cube melts more quickly. Conclusion: Salt melts ice.

WEEK 4

Concept

Water evaporates, or becomes a gas, when it is heated.

Where Did the Water Go?

Science Objective:
To help students understand that evaporation is the result of water becoming water vapor, which is a gas

Science Vocabulary:
air, droplets, evaporate, gas, puddle, water vapor

Day 1 SKILLS

Physical Science
- Observe and describe properties of objects
- Understand that water can be a solid, a liquid, or a gas

Literacy

Oral Language Development
- Respond orally to simple questions

Comprehension
- Make connections using illustrations, prior knowledge, or real-life experiences
- Answer questions about key details in a text read aloud

Introducing the Concept

A day or two before the lesson, have students observe as you fill a clear plastic cup with water and use a marker to indicate the waterline. Set the cup in a sunny window or near a warm air vent. On the day of this lesson, have students note that there is now less water in the cup. Say:

The sun made the water in the cup warm. When water gets warm enough, it turns into tiny drops of water that go into the air. We say the water **evaporates***, or turns from a liquid into a* **gas***.*

- *Imagine you are coming out of a swimming pool on a summer day. You are dripping wet. What form is the water in?* (liquid)
- *What if you were to sit in the sun afterward? You would soon be dry. Where did the water go?* (into the air) *Yes, the water* **evaporated***. It became a* **gas***.*

Listening to the Story

Distribute the Day 1 activity page to each student. Say: *I'm going to read you a story that explains how the sun's heat evaporates water in rain puddles.*

This morning it was raining, so Hector put on his rain boots. When he got to school, he splashed in the puddles while he waited for the bell to ring. Soon, the sun came out. Before recess, Mrs. Chen asked Hector to check the playground for puddles. They were gone! Mrs. Chen explained that the water in the puddles had evaporated. The heat from the sun changed the liquid water into gas, or tiny drops, that had spread into the air. The children didn't need to wear rain boots to go on the playground!

Confirming Understanding

Distribute crayons. Develop the science concept by asking questions about the story. Ask:

- *Where did the water in the puddles come from?* (rain) *Make an* **X** *on a puddle.*
- *What happened when the sun came out?* (The puddles evaporated.) *Draw a circle around the sun.*
- *Where did the water go?* (into the air)

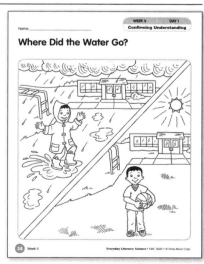

Day 1 picture

Physical Science

- Observe and describe properties of objects
- Understand that water can be a solid, a liquid, or a gas

Literacy

Oral Language Development

- Use traditional structures, such as chronological order, to convey information

Comprehension

- Recall details
- Make connections using illustrations, prior knowledge, or real-life experiences

Reinforcing the Concept

Reread the Day 1 story. Then reinforce this week's science concept. Say:

In the story, the water in the puddles evaporated. Where did the water go? (into the air) *Water that turns into tiny little droplets and goes into the air is called gas.*

Distribute the Day 2 activity and crayons. Say:

- *Look at the pictures. Which picture shows what happened first in the story?* (Hector splashing in puddles while it is raining) *Draw a line from that picture to the number 1.*

- *Which picture shows what happened next?* (sun shining; puddles beginning to evaporate; gas rising) *Draw a line from that picture to the number 2.*

- *Which picture shows what happened third?* (Hector on the dry playground) *Draw a line from that picture to the number 3.*

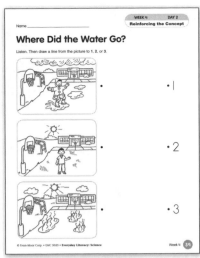

Day 2 activity

Physical Science

- Observe and describe properties of objects
- Understand that water can be a solid, a liquid, or a gas

Literacy

Oral Language Development

- Use traditional structures, such as cause and effect, to convey information

Comprehension

- Make connections using illustrations, prior knowledge, or real-life experiences

Developing the Concept

To introduce the activity, say:

When water gets warm, it evaporates. It changes from a liquid to a gas. The hotter the water is, the faster it evaporates.

Distribute the Day 3 activity and crayons. Say:

- *Point to picture 1. It shows a glass of water. If nobody drinks it, the water will start to evaporate. It will turn into a gas. Which picture shows that?* (the glass that has less water) *Draw a line to the picture.*

- *Point to picture 2. It shows a rain puddle. When the sun comes out, the puddle will evaporate. Which picture shows that?* (the dry sidewalk) *Draw a line to the picture.*

- *Point to picture 3. It shows a pot of water that is cooking on the stove. Which picture shows what will soon happen?* (the pot that is steaming) *Draw a line to the picture.*

- *Point to picture 4. It shows a boy dripping wet in a pool. Which picture shows what will happen if he sits out in the sun?* (the boy lying on the towel) *Draw a line to the picture.*

Day 3 activity

Physical Science
• Observe and describe
  properties of objects
• Understand that water
  can be a solid, a liquid,
  or a gas

Literacy

**Oral Language
Development**
• Use traditional structures,
  such as chronological
  order, to convey
  information

Comprehension
• Make connections using
  illustrations, prior
  knowledge, or real-life
  experiences

Applying the Concept

Introduce the activity by saying:

> *Heat from the sun makes water evaporate.
> The water changes from liquid to gas. The
> water vapor goes into the air.*

Distribute the Day 4 activity and crayons. Say:

- *One day, Emma filled a clear plastic glass
  with water. She used a marker to make a
  line on the glass at the top of the water.
  Emma set the glass in a sunny window.
  Then she checked it each day to see what
  happened to the water.*

- *Look at the pictures. Which picture shows
  what happened first?* (Emma filling a glass)
  Draw a line from that picture to number 1.

- *Which picture shows what happened second?* (Emma marking the
  glass) *Draw a line from that picture to number 2.*

- *Which picture shows what happened third?* (Emma putting the glass
  in a sunny window) *Draw a line from that picture to number 3.*

- *Which picture shows what happened fourth?* (glass with less water
  in it) *Draw a line from that picture to number 4.*

Day 4 activity

Physical Science
• Observe and describe
  properties of objects
• Understand that water
  can be a solid, a liquid,
  or a gas

**Scientific Thinking
& Inquiry**
• Gather and record
  information through
  simple observations
  and investigations

**Home–School
Connection p. 42**
Spanish version
available (see p. 2)

Hands-on Science Activity

Reinforce this week's science concept with
the following hands-on activity:

Materials: one clear plastic cup per student;
black marker; water

Activity: Give each student a cup and have
them pour some water into it. Then help them
draw a line on the outside of the cup to mark
the waterline. Tell students that they will place
their cups of water in different areas of the room
(some that receive sunlight and some that do not),
and see where the water evaporates the fastest. Say:

> *You know that heat from the sun evaporates water. We are going
> to check our cups every two days to see what happens to the
> water and draw a new line on our cups to show if any water has
> evaporated.*

Have students observe their cups of water. Make a chart and record whose
water evaporated the fastest. Ask:

> *Why do you think some cups of water evaporated faster than others?*
> (They were put in warmer places; They were put nearer the sunlight.)

Name _____

Where Did the Water Go?

Everyday Literacy: Science • EMC 5025 • © Evan-Moor Corp.

Name _____

Where Did the Water Go?

Listen. Then draw a line from the picture to **1**, **2**, or **3**.

•   •|

•   •2

•   •3

Name _____

Where Did the Water Go?

Listen and follow the directions. Draw lines to match.

1  •   •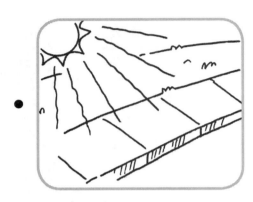

2  •   •

3  •   •

4  •   •

Name _____

Where Did the Water Go?

Listen. Then draw a line from the picture to **1**, **2**, **3**, or **4**.

   •

•1

   •

•2

   •

•3

   •

•4

Name _____

What I Learned

What to Do
Have your child look at the pictures below. Ask him or her to tell you how the pictures are different. Then ask, *How did the puddles evaporate?* (The heat from the sun changed the liquid water into gas, or tiny drops, that spread into the air.)

Science Concept: Water evaporates when it is heated.

To Parents
This week your child learned that water changes to water vapor (a gas) when heated.

What to Do Next
Have your child fill a small clear plastic container with water. Use a marker to show the waterline. Place the container by a heating vent or in a sunny window. Have your child check the water level each day.

Everyday Literacy: Science • EMC 5025 • © Evan-Moor Corp.

Wheels Do the Work

Concept

A wheel and axle is a simple machine that makes work easier.

Science Objective:
To introduce students to the idea that wheels make work easier for people

Science Vocabulary:
pull, push, wheel, work

Day 1
SKILLS

Physical Science
- Identify tools and simple machines used for a specific purpose

Literacy

Oral Language
- Respond orally to simple questions

Comprehension
- Make connections using illustrations, prior knowledge, or real-life experiences
- Answer questions about key details in a text read aloud

Introducing the Concept

Display a toy car and an eraser. Ask:

- *Which of these do you think is easier to push?* (the car) *Why?* (It has wheels.)

- *Which of these do you think is easier to pull?* (the car) *Why?* (It has wheels.) *Yes, wheels make it easier to move things.*

- *Do any of your toys have wheels?* (students respond) *Does your toy move fast or slow?* (students respond)

Listening to the Story

Distribute the Day 1 activity page. Say: *Listen and look at the picture as I read you a story about brothers who use wheels to make work easier.*

One day, Carlos and Gabriel were helping their dad load things into his pickup truck. They were going to take everything to the recycling center. "Get that big box of newspapers and bring it over here," said their dad. Carlos and Gabriel ran into the garage to get the box. The boys pushed and pushed the box, but it would hardly move. Then Gabriel had an idea. He got his wagon. The boys asked their dad to lift the box into the wagon. The wagon was easy to pull because it had wheels. "That wagon sure made work easier!" said their dad. The boys thought it made work more fun, too!

Confirming Understanding

Distribute crayons. Reinforce the science concept by asking questions about the story. Ask:

- *What did the boys have to do?* (bring a box of newspapers over to the truck) *Color the truck green.*

- *What happened when the boys tried to push the box?* (It wouldn't move.) *Why?* (It was heavy.) *Color the box brown.*

- *What happened when the boys put the box into the wagon?* (They could pull the wagon and move the box.) *Color the wagon red. Why was it easy to pull the wagon?* (because it had wheels) *Color one wheel black.*

Day 1 picture

Physical Science

• Identify tools and simple machines used for a specific purpose

Literacy

Oral Language Development

• Respond orally to simple questions

Comprehension

• Recall details

• Make connections using illustrations, prior knowledge, or real-life experiences

Reinforcing the Concept

Reread the Day 1 story. Then reinforce this week's science concept by guiding a discussion about the story. Say:

We learned that wheels make work easier. How did wheels make work easier for Carlos and Gabriel? (Wheels made it easier for the boys to move the box.)

Distribute the Day 2 activity and crayons. Say:

• *Point to box 1. Is this person using wheels to make work easier? Color the happy face for* **yes** *or the sad face for* **no**. (yes) *What work is this person doing?* (driving a delivery truck)

• *Point to box 2. Is this person using wheels to make work easier? Color the happy face for* **yes** *or the sad face for* **no**. (no)

• *Point to box 3. Is this person using wheels to make work easier? Color the happy face for* **yes** *or the sad face for* **no**. (yes) *What work is this boy doing?* (rolling his chair into school)

• *Point to box 4. Is this person using wheels to make work easier? Color the happy face for* **yes** *or the sad face for* **no**. (no)

Day 2 activity

Physical Science

• Identify tools and simple machines used for a specific purpose

Literacy

Oral Language Development

• Name and describe pictured objects

Comprehension

• Make connections using illustrations, prior knowledge, or real-life experiences

Applying the Concept

To introduce the activity, guide a discussion that helps students recall the Day 1 story. Say:

First, Carlos and Gabriel tried to push the newspapers in a box. Why did the wagon work better? (because it had wheels)

Distribute the Day 3 activity and crayons. Say:

• *Look at the picture. Circle all the people who are using wheels to make their work easier. Put your crayon down when you are finished.*

Allow students time to complete the activity. After they are finished, say:

• *Let's talk about the pictures you circled. Did you circle the mom pushing the baby? How do wheels make her work easier?* (She does not need to carry the baby.)

• *Who else uses wheels to move something heavy?* (boy with wagon; gardener with wheelbarrow)

• *Who uses wheels as transportation?* (child on bike; people on bus)

Day 3 activity

Physical Science
- Identify tools and simple machines used for a specific purpose

Literacy

Oral Language Development
- Name and describe pictured objects
- Respond orally to simple questions

Comprehension
- Make connections using illustrations, prior knowledge, or real-life experiences

Applying the Concept

Introduce the activity by saying:

Wheels make work easier. A bike has wheels that turn, making it easier to move from place to place. A wagon also makes it easier to move things from place to place.

Distribute the Day 4 activity and crayons. Say:

- *Point to the first picture. It shows children walking to school. What could help them get to school?* (school bus with wheels) *Draw a line to the picture of a school bus.*

- *Point to picture 2. What does it show?* (a man shopping for groceries) *What could make it easier for him to shop?* (shopping cart with wheels) *Draw a line to the picture that shows a shopping cart.*

- *Point to picture 3. What does it show?* (a girl carrying a lot of dolls) *What could help her carry her dolls?* (a wagon with wheels) *Draw a line to the picture that shows a wagon with wheels.*

Day 4 activity

Physical Science
- Identify tools and simple machines used for a specific purpose

Scientific Thinking & Inquiry
- Experiment with simple machines
- Gather and record information through simple observations and investigations

Home–School Connection p. 50
Spanish version available (see p. 2)

Hands-on Science Activity

Reinforce this week's science concept with the following hands-on activity:

Materials: empty spools of thread; plastic drinking straws; play dough; rolling pin

Activity: To introduce the activity, show students the rolling pin. Ask them what it is used for (to roll out dough). Explain that a rolling pin is a kind of wheel even though it doesn't look like one. To help students understand this, have them each make a "rolling pin" from a spool and a straw by poking the straw through the hole in the spool. Then give each student a small piece of play dough to roll out with his or her rolling pin.

Next, have students each use two spools and a straw to make a set of wheels. Show students how to put the spools on the ends of the straw. Apply play dough to the tips of the straw to prevent the spools from sliding off. Then have students try out their "wheels" by pushing them across the floor with a partner, to see how far the spools will roll.

Wheels Do the Work

Name _____

Wheels Do the Work

Listen. Color the happy face for **yes**. Color the sad face for **no**.

Name _____

Wheels Do the Work

Circle the people who are using wheels to make their work easier.

Everyday Literacy: Science • EMC 5025 • © Evan-Moor Corp.

Name _____

Wheels Do the Work

Draw a line to match.

1  •   •

2  •   •

3  •   •

Name _____

What I Learned

What to Do

Have your child look at the picture below and circle the people who are using wheels to make their work easier. Then discuss which things have wheels and how they make work easier.

Science Concept: A wheel and axle is a simple machine that makes work easier.

To Parents

This week your child learned that wheels help make work easier.

What to Do Next

Help your child find items around your house that have wheels. Talk about how the wheels make work easier. For example, ask, *Do the wheels make the toy car move faster? Do the wheels help the chair move easily?*

Concept

Scientists use certain words to describe the position of objects.

Tell Where It Is

Science Objective:
To help students learn to use positional words and relative terms

Science Vocabulary:
above, below, in, inside, next to, on, outside, over, under

Day 1
SKILLS

Investigation
• Understand that the position of objects can be described
• Identify and describe objects in a given position

Literacy

Oral Language Development
• Respond orally to simple questions

Comprehension
• Make connections using illustrations, prior knowledge, or real-life experiences
• Answer questions about key details in a text read aloud

Introducing the Concept

Before the lesson, place an object on a table, place another one under the table, and place a third next to the table. Say:

*Look around the room. We can use words such as **on**, **in**, **next to**, **above**, **below**, **over**, **under**, **inside**, and **outside** to tell where things are.*

• *Look at that table. What is **on** the table?* (students respond)

• *What is **under** the table?* (students respond)

• *What is **next to** the table?* (students respond)

Continue the discussion using **inside**, **outside**, **above**, and **below**.

Listening to the Story

Distribute the Day 1 activity page. Say: *Listen and look at the picture as I read a story about a girl who keeps toys in many places.*

---

    *Hailey has a lot of toys! They are all around her room. There are toys **above** her bed. There are toys **under** her bed. There are even toys **in** her bed! Hailey likes having toys everywhere. She keeps her teacups **on** her table. She puts her teapot **next to** her teacups. She keeps her dolls **inside** her dollhouse. She keeps their little pink car parked right **outside** the dollhouse. You can find a toy almost anywhere you look—except the toy box!*

Confirming Understanding

Distribute crayons or markers. Reinforce the science concept by asking:

• *Are there toys **above** Hailey's bed?* (yes) *Make a red dot on one of the toys above Hailey's bed.*

• *Are there toys **in** Hailey's bed?* (yes) *What are they?* (a teddy bear and a doll) *Color the teddy bear brown.*

• *What is **next to** Hailey's teacups?* (the teapot) *Color the teapot green.*

• *What is **inside** Hailey's toy box?* (nothing) *Draw your favorite toy inside the toy box.*

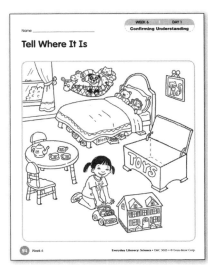

Day 1 picture

Day 2
SKILLS

Investigation
- Understand that the position of objects can be described
- Identify and describe objects in a given position

Literacy

Oral Language Development
- Respond orally to simple questions

Comprehension
- Recall details

Reinforcing the Concept

Reread the Day 1 story. Then reinforce this week's science concept by guiding a discussion about the story. Say:

Our story was about where Hailey keeps her toys. Words like in, on, next to, and above tell where Hailey's toys are.

Distribute the Day 2 activity and crayons. Say:

- *Listen carefully and follow my directions. Point to box 1. Is the teddy bear under this chair? Color the happy face for yes or the sad face for no.* (no)
- *Point to box 2. Is the horse inside the barn? Color the happy face for yes or the sad face for no.* (yes) *Where is the cow?* (outside the barn; next to the barn)
- *Look at box 3. Is the cloud above the house? Color the happy face for yes or the sad face for no.* (yes)
- *Look at box 4. Is the teapot below the shelf? Color the happy face for yes or the sad face for no.* (no)

Day 2 activity

Day 3
SKILLS

Investigation
- Understand that the position of objects can be described
- Identify and describe objects in a given position

Literacy

Oral Language Development
- Respond orally to simple questions

Comprehension
- Recall details

Applying the Concept

Introduce the activity by saying:

Words help us understand where things are.

- *What is above you?* (students respond)
- *What is next to you?* (students respond)

Distribute the Day 3 activity and crayons. Say:

- *Look at this picture. Point to the tree. What is inside the tree?* (a nest; little birds) *The nest is inside the tree. Where are the little birds?* (in the nest) *Yes, the birds are in the nest. Color one bird yellow.*
- *Point to the tree branch. What animal is on the branch?* (an owl) *Yes, an owl is sitting on the branch. Circle the owl.*
- *Point to the squirrel. What is the squirrel next to?* (the tree) *Yes, the squirrel is next to the tree. Draw a line from the squirrel to the tree.*
- *Look at the picture. Do you see any animals below ground?* (yes) *Yes, there is a gopher below ground. Color the gopher brown.*
- *What is above the gopher?* (a flower) *Yes, a flower is above the gopher. Draw a line from the gopher to the flower.*

Day 3 activity

Everyday Literacy: Science • EMC 5025 • © Evan-Moor Corp.

Day 4
SKILLS

Investigation
- Understand that the position of objects can be described
- Identify and describe objects in a given position

Literacy

Oral Language Development
- Respond orally to simple questions
- Use new vocabulary

Comprehension
- Recall details

Applying the Concept

Review this week's science concept by saying:

We can use words that tell where things are in our classroom.

- *Let's use the word **on**. Look for an object that is **on** a table. Say: The _____ is on the table. (students respond)*

- *Let's use the words **next to**. Look for an object that is **next to** the door. Repeat this sentence after me: The _____ is next to the door. (students respond)*

Then distribute the Day 4 activity and crayons. Say:

- *Point to box 1. Where is the rabbit? (**on** the bench) What is **above** the rabbit? (a bird) Draw a sun **above** the bird.*

- *Point to box 2. Where is the boy? (**in** the pool) What is **next to** the boy? (a ball) Draw another ball **on** the grass.*

- *Point to box 3. Where is the bird? (**inside** the birdhouse; **above** the cat) Where is the cat? (**under** the birdhouse; **next to** the birdhouse) Draw a worm **next to** the cat.*

- *Point to box 4. The goat walked **over** the bridge. Draw a line **over** the bridge. Now look **under** the bridge. What do you see? (a frog) Is the bridge **above** the frog or **below** the frog? (above) Draw a circle around the frog.*

Day 4 activity

Day 5
SKILLS

Investigation
- Understand that the position of objects can be described
- Identify and describe objects in a given position

Literacy

Oral Language Development
- Give and follow directions
- Use new vocabulary

Home–School Connection p. 58
Spanish version available (see p. 2)

Hands-on Science Activity

Reinforce this week's science concept with the following hands-on activity:

Materials: small colored cubes or blocks; one 12-inch length of yarn per student

Preparation: Provide each student with a length of yarn and 3 or 4 cubes.

Activity: Introduce the activity by saying:

People use certain words to tell where things are. I am going to tell you where to place the yarn and the cubes. Listen carefully.

- *Place a red cube **next to** a yellow cube. Place a green cube **on** a red cube.*

- *Make a circle with your yarn. Place a blue cube **inside** the circle. Place a green cube **outside** the circle.*

Direct pairs of students to take turns giving directions to each other. Encourage them to use the vocabulary words they have learned. List the words on the board or a chart for students to refer to as they work together.

Name _____

Tell Where It Is

Name _____

Tell Where It Is

Listen. Color the happy face for **yes**. Color the sad face for **no**.

Name _____

Tell Where It Is

Listen and follow the directions.

| on | in | next to | below | above |

Name _____

Tell Where It Is

Listen and follow the directions.

Name _____

What I Learned

What to Do

Have your child look at the picture. Ask him or her to point to the toys and tell where they are in the bedroom by using positional words such as *above*, *below*, *in*, *on*, *inside*, *outside*, *over*, *under*, and *next to*. Then have your child color the picture.

Science Concept: Scientists describe the position of objects.

To Parents
This week your child listened to a story about a girl who has her toys all around her room, except where they belong.

What to Do Next

Play a directions game with your child, using three toys. Give directions such as, *Put the car **inside** the sand pail. Put the sand pail **next to** the doll.* Then let your child give you directions.

Everyday Literacy: Science • EMC 5025 • © Evan-Moor Corp.

Concept

We use our five senses to learn about the world.

My Five Senses

Science Objective:
To help students understand that they have five senses that help them explore the world around them

Science Vocabulary:
ears, eyes, feel, hands, hear, mouth, nose, see, smell, taste, touch

Day 1 SKILLS

Life Science
- Associate each of the five senses with a part of the body
- Understand that our five senses help us learn about the world around us

Literacy

Oral Language Development
- Respond orally to simple questions

Comprehension
- Make connections using illustrations, prior knowledge, or real-life experiences
- Answer questions about key details in a text read aloud
- Make inferences and draw conclusions

Introducing the Concept

Tell students that our five senses help us learn about the world. Point to each body part as you refer to it, saying:

- *We use our eyes to see. We use our ears to hear. We use our hands to touch. We use our mouth to taste. We use our nose to smell.*
- *Point to your eyes. What do you use your eyes to do?* (see) *Point to your ears. What do you use your ears to do?* (hear) *Repeat for* **hands**, **mouth**, *and* **nose**.

Listening to the Story

Direct students' attention to the Day 1 page. Say: *Listen and look at the picture as I read a story about a boy who uses his five senses.*

---

*My grandma and grandpa live in a cabin at the lake. There's so much to see and do there. I use all of my senses. My ears **hear** the birds chirping early in the morning. My eyes **see** the sun coming up over the lake. My nose **smells** the pancakes Grandma is cooking for breakfast. I pour maple syrup all over the pancakes and stuff big bites into my mouth. Yum! They **taste** sweet and buttery, so I use my finger to wipe up every drop. The syrup makes my fingers **feel** sticky, but it makes my tummy feel full!*

Confirming Understanding

Distribute crayons or markers. Reinforce the science concept by asking:

- *What body part did the boy use to **hear** the birds chirping?* (ears) *Circle the boy's ear.*
- *What body part did he use to **see** the sun coming up?* (eyes) *Make an **X** on his eye.*
- *What body part did he use to **smell** the pancakes?* (nose) *Make a dot on his nose.*
- *What body part did he use to **taste** the pancakes and syrup?* (mouth) *Make a red dot on his mouth.*
- *What body part did he use to **touch** the syrup?* (finger; hands) *Circle his hand.*

Day 1 picture

Day 2
SKILLS

Life Science

• Associate each of the five senses with a part of the body

• Understand that our five senses help us learn about the world around us

Literacy

Oral Language Development

• Respond orally to simple questions

Comprehension

• Recall details

• Make inferences and draw conclusions

Reinforcing the Concept

Reread the Day 1 story. Then reinforce this week's science concept by reviewing:

The boy in our story used his five senses. What were they? (seeing, hearing, smelling, etc.)

Distribute the Day 2 activity and crayons. Say:

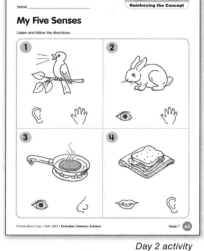

Day 2 activity

• *Point to box 1. The big picture shows a bird chirping. Which body part do you use to hear a bird chirping, your ears or your hands?* (ears) *Draw a line from the bird to the ear.*

• *Point to box 2. The big picture shows a soft bunny. Which body part would you use to touch a bunny's soft fur, your eyes or your hands?* (hands) *Draw a line from the bunny to the hand.*

• *Point to box 3. The big picture show a pancake cooking. Which body part do you use to smell pancakes cooking, your eyes or your nose?* (nose) *Draw a line from the pancake to the nose.*

• *Point to box 4. The big picture shows a sandwich. Which body part do you use to taste a sandwich, your mouth or your ears?* (mouth) *Draw a line from the sandwich to the mouth.*

Day 3
SKILLS

Life Science

• Associate each of the five senses with a part of the body

• Understand that our five senses help us learn about the world around us

Literacy

Oral Language Development

• Respond orally to simple questions

Comprehension

• Recall details

• Make connections using illustrations, prior knowledge, or real-life experiences

Applying the Concept

Distribute the Day 3 activity and say:

We use our senses to find out about our world. Help Ally use her senses.

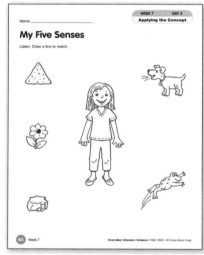

Day 3 activity

• *Ally hears barking. Which animal can bark?* (dog) *What body part does Ally use to hear?* (ears) *Draw a line from one of Ally's ears to the dog.*

• *Ally smells something sweet. Which picture shows something that smells sweet?* (flower) *What body part does Ally use to smell?* (nose) *Draw a line from Ally's nose to the flower.*

• *Ally sees something hopping. Which animal can hop?* (frog) *What body part does Ally use to see?* (eyes) *Draw a line from one of Ally's eyes to the frog.*

• *Ally feels something hard and rough. Which picture shows something hard and rough?* (rock) *What body part does Ally use to feel or touch?* (hands) *Draw a line from one of Ally's hands to the rock.*

• *Ally tastes something salty. Which picture shows something that tastes salty?* (tortilla chip) *What body part does Ally use to taste?* (mouth) *Draw a line from Ally's mouth to the chip.*

Life Science
- Associate each of the five senses with a part of the body
- Understand that our five senses help us learn about the world around us

Literacy

Oral Language Development
- Respond orally to simple questions

Comprehension
- Make connections using illustrations, prior knowledge, or real-life experiences

Applying the Concept

Distribute the Day 4 activity and crayons. Then guide students through the activity by saying:

Day 4 activity

- *Point to the nose. What do you use your nose for?* (to smell) *Point to the cloud, the fish, and the flower. Which of these could you smell?* (fish, flower) *Draw a line under the things you could smell.*

- *Point to the ear. What do you use your ears for?* (to hear) *Point to the pictures of the alarm clock ringing, the girl whistling, and the snowman melting. Which of these could you hear?* (alarm clock, girl) *Draw a line under the things you could hear.*

- *Point to the hand. Do you use your hands to touch?* (yes) *Point to the pencil, the fish, and the sun. Which of these could you touch?* (pencil, the fish) *Draw a line under the things you could touch.*

- *Point to the mouth. Do you use your mouth to taste?* (yes) *Point to the cookie, the flower, and the lemonade. Which of these could you taste?* (cookie, lemonade) *Draw a line under the things you could taste.*

- *Point to the eye. What do you use your eyes for?* (to see) *Point to the cloud, the television, and the banana. Which of these could you see?* (all of them) *Draw a line under the things you could see.*

Life Science
- Associate each of the five senses with a part of the body

Literacy

Oral Language Development
- Use descriptive language

Scientific Thinking & Inquiry
- Gather and record information through simple observations and investigations
- Record observations and data with pictures and other symbols

Home–School Connection p. 66
Spanish version available (see p. 2)

Hands-on Science Activity

Reinforce this week's science concept with the following hands-on activity:

Materials: a shoe box for each group of students; a variety of objects that students can see, hear, touch, smell, and taste, such as bells, blocks, bag of beans; scraps of velvet and wool, cotton balls, sandpaper, aluminum foil, smooth and bumpy rocks; cinnamon sticks, crayons, chocolate, flowers, banana, orange; crackers, popcorn, jelly beans, celery

Preparation: Divide items among the shoe boxes, making sure that each box contains items from each sense group. Make a chart on the board that includes a row for each sense. Divide students into groups.

Activity: Give each group a shoe box. Then introduce the activity by saying:

We are going to use our body parts to learn more about the objects in the shoe boxes. We will talk about how an object looks, feels, smells, tastes, and sounds. Then we will record what we learned about each item.

Have each group talk about the items in their box and which sense they used to learn more about each item. Model using descriptive words such as *smooth, rough, sweet, salty,* etc.

Name _____

My Five Senses

Name _____

My Five Senses

Listen and follow the directions.

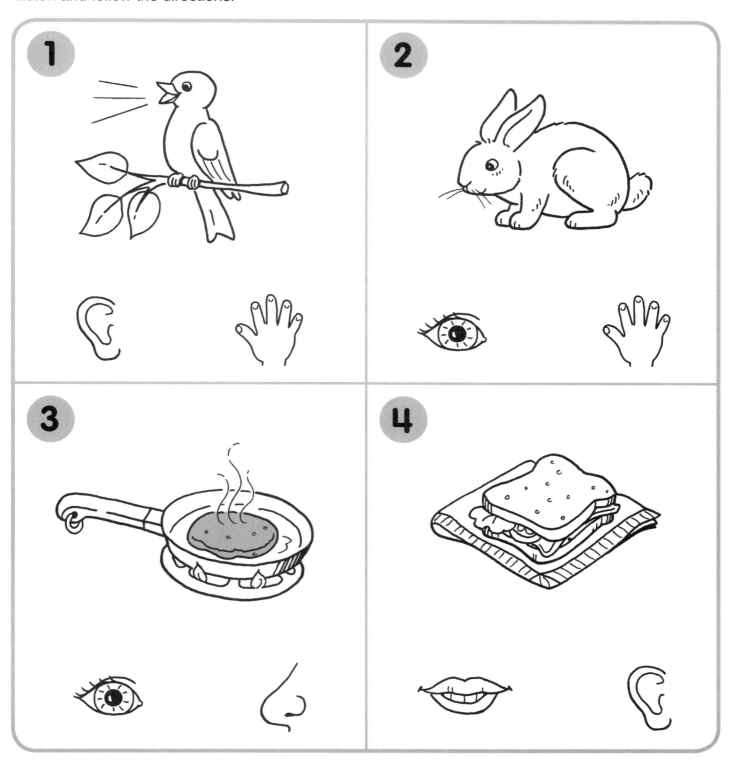

Name _____

My Five Senses

Listen. Draw a line to match.

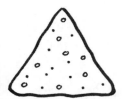

Name _____

My Five Senses

Listen and follow the directions.

Name _____

What I Learned

What to Do

Have your child look at the first picture in each row. Ask: *Which of the five senses does it represent?* Then have your child circle the pictures in each row that he or she can identify by using that particular sense.

Science Concept: We use our five senses to find out about the world.

To Parents
This week your child learned that our senses help us investigate and learn about the world.

What to Do Next

Help your child find magazine pictures to represent each of the five senses: seeing, hearing, touching, smelling, and tasting.

Everyday Literacy: Science • EMC 5025 • © Evan-Moor Corp.

What Plants Need

Science Objective:
To help students understand that plants are living things that need soil, air, water, and sunlight

Science Vocabulary:
air, investigate, soil, sunlight, water

Day 1
SKILLS

Life Science
• Understand that plants, animals, and people are living things that have basic needs

Literacy

Oral Language Development
• Respond orally to simple questions

Comprehension
• Make connections using illustrations, prior knowledge, or real-life experiences
• Answer questions about key details in a text read aloud
• Make inferences and draw conclusions

Introducing the Concept

Distribute the Day 1 activity page. Point to the plants in the picture. Say:

• *Plants are living things. Plants need four things to live and grow: soil, air, water, and sunlight.*

• *What do you think would happen to a plant if one of those things were missing?* (students respond)

• *One way to find out is to take one of those things away and watch what happens to the plant. You can* **investigate** *what happens.*

Listening to the Story

Redirect students' attention to the Day 1 page. Say: *Listen and look at the picture as I read a story about children who learn about what plants need.*

My class decided to investigate what plants need to live and grow. We gave one plant soil, air, and water, but it did not get sunlight. We put a paper bag over it and put it in a dark closet. We gave another plant soil, air, and sunlight, but we didn't water it for two weeks. We gave the third plant everything—soil, air, water, and sunlight. Guess what happened? The plant without sunlight got droopy and yellow. The plant without water dried up and turned brown. The plant that got everything stayed green and healthy; it even grew new leaves!

Confirming Understanding

Distribute crayons. Reinforce the science concept by asking questions about the story. Ask:

• *What happened to the plant that was covered up and didn't get any sunlight?* (droopy, yellow) *Circle the plant that was covered up.*

• *What happened to the plant that didn't get water?* (dried up, brown) *Make an X on the plant that went without water.*

• *What did the healthy plant get?* (soil, air, water, sunlight) *Color the healthy plant green.*

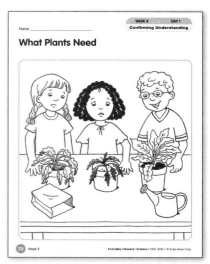

Day 1 picture

Life Science
• Understand that plants, animals, and people are living things that have basic needs

Literacy

Oral Language Development
• Use traditional structures, such as cause and effect, to convey information

Comprehension
• Recall details
• Make inferences and draw conclusions

Reinforcing the Concept

Reread the Day 1 story. Then reinforce this week's science concept by guiding a discussion about the story. Say:

Our story named four things that plants need: soil, air, water, and sunlight.

Distribute the Day 2 activity and crayons. Say:

• *Point to box 1. Plants need water. Did this plant have water? Color the happy face for **yes** or the sad face for **no**.* (no)

• *Point to box 2. Did this plant have water? Color the happy face for **yes** or the sad face for **no**.* (yes)

• *Point to box 3. Plants need sunlight. Did this plant have sunlight? Color the happy face for **yes** or the sad face for **no**.* (yes)

• *Point to box 4. Plants need soil. Did this plant have soil? Color the happy face for **yes** or the sad face for **no**.* (no)

Day 2 activity

Life Science
• Understand that plants, animals, and people are living things that have basic needs

Literacy

Oral Language Development
• Respond orally to simple questions

Comprehension
• Make inferences and draw conclusions

Applying the Concept

Distribute the Day 3 activity and crayons. Then introduce the activity by reviewing:

Plants are living things that need soil, air, water, and sunlight in order to live and grow.

• *Look at the picture. What is the girl growing in her garden? (plants) Color one plant green.*

• *Do the plants look healthy? (yes) The plants are growing in the soil. The soil keeps the plants healthy. Color the soil brown.*

• *Air is everywhere even though we cannot see it. Plants need air to be healthy. Draw a bird flying through the air.*

• *What else do plants need to be healthy? (sunlight, water) Draw a sun in the sky. Draw water spraying from the hose.*

• *Do these plants have everything they need to be healthy? (yes)*

Day 3 activity

Have students draw colorful flowers growing on the plants. Then have them finish coloring the picture.

Extending the Concept

Distribute the Day 4 activity and crayons. Then introduce the activity by saying:

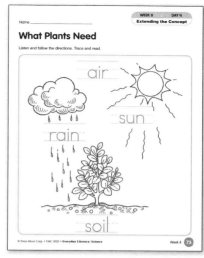

The children in our story learned that plants are living things that need soil, air, water, and sunlight. This picture shows a plant that lives and grows outdoors.

- *Look at the picture. Air is all around us, but we cannot see it. Air helps plants grow and be healthy. Where is the air in this picture?* (all around) *Find the word **air** at the top of the picture. Say **air**.* (air) *Trace the letters that spell **air**. Put your crayon down when you are finished.*

Day 4 activity

- *Point to the cloud. A cloud has rainwater in it. Rain helps plants grow and be healthy. Put your crayon on the word **rain**. Say **rain**.* (rain) *Trace the letters that spell **rain**. Put your crayon down when you are finished.*

- *Now point to the sun. Sunlight helps plants grow and be healthy. Put your crayon on the word **sun**. Say **sun**.* (sun) *Trace the letters that spell **sun**. Put your crayon down when you are finished.*

- *Now point to the soil. Soil helps plants grow and be healthy. Say **soil**.* (soil) *Trace the letters that spell **soil**. When you are finished tracing, color the picture.*

Hands-on Science Activity

Reinforce this week's science concept with the following hands-on activity:

Materials: two identical small green plants

Activity: Place the plants in a sunny window. Say:

You know that plants need soil, air, water, and sunlight. What do you think will happen if we water only one of these plants? Will both plants grow? Will they be the same or different?

Over the next few weeks, water one plant as needed, but do not water the other. Every few days, have students examine the plants and describe what they see. End the investigation by displaying the unhealthy plant. Ask:

What happened to this plant? Why does it look so bad? (It didn't get any water; Plants need water.)

Have students draw pictures of the healthy and unhealthy plants.

What Plants Need

Name _____

What Plants Need

Listen. Color the happy face for **yes**. Color the sad face for **no**.

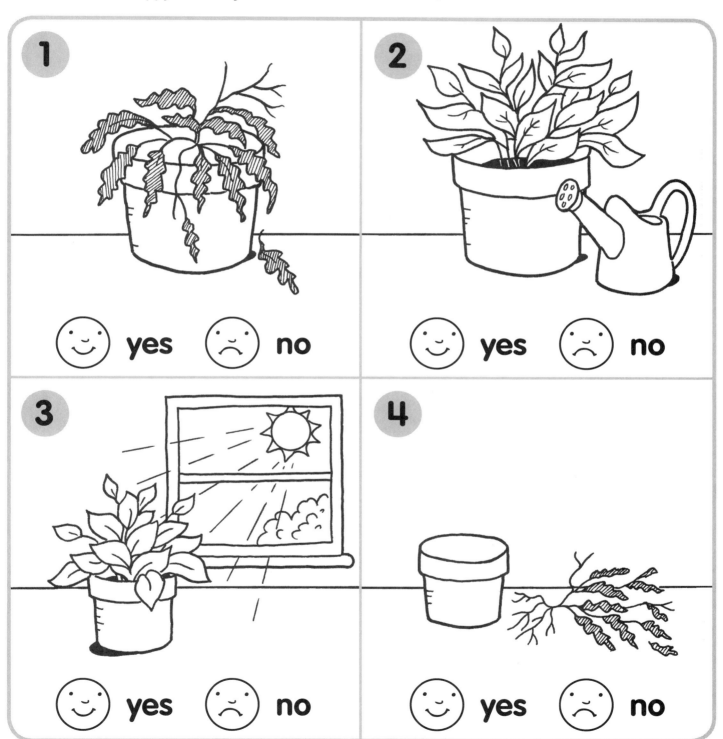

1
☺ yes ☹ no

2
☺ yes ☹ no

3
☺ yes ☹ no

4
☺ yes ☹ no

Name _____

What Plants Need

Listen and follow the directions. Draw flowers and color the picture.

Name _____

What Plants Need

Listen and follow the directions. Trace and read.

air

sun

rain

soil

Name _____

What I Learned

What to Do

Have your child look at the picture below. Talk about the things a plant needs in order to grow (soil, air, water, sunlight). Have your child point to the plants that didn't get all the things they needed, and the one that did. Then have your child color the picture.

WEEK 8

Home–School Connection

Science Concept: Living things have basic needs.

To Parents

This week your child learned about what plants need to live and grow.

What to Do Next

Help your child look through magazines to find and cut out pictures of plants to glue onto a sheet of drawing paper. Then have your child draw in details such as soil, sun, and a water source.

Everyday Literacy: Science • EMC 5025 • © Evan-Moor Corp.

What Animals Need

Science Objective:
To help students understand that animals are living things that need food,
water, air, and shelter

Science Vocabulary:
air, food, shelter, water, wild

Day 1
SKILLS

Life Science
• Understand that plants,
animals, and people are
living things that have
basic needs

Literacy

**Oral Language
Development**
• Respond orally to simple
questions

Comprehension
• Make connections
using illustrations, prior
knowledge, or real-life
experiences
• Answer questions about
key details in a text read
aloud
• Make inferences and
draw conclusions

Introducing the Concept

Activate prior knowledge by asking students who have pets to tell about how
their family takes care of the pet and what their pet needs. Say:

• *Pets are animals and are living things. Animals need four things
to live and grow: food, water, air, and shelter.*

• *What kinds of food do your pets like to eat?* (students respond)

• ***Shelter** is a place where an animal can go to be safe from weather or
danger. Our pets live in our homes for shelter. Where do you think wild
animals go for shelter?* (in trees, in the ground, under rocks, etc.)

Listening to the Story

Distribute the Day 1 activity page. Say: *Listen and look at the picture as I read
you a story about taking care of a class pet.*

---

   *Animals are living things. They need food, water, air, and shelter
to live and grow. Our class pet, Miss Bunny, needs all those things.
A wild rabbit finds its own food, water, and shelter. But Miss Bunny is
a pet. We give her fresh hay and carrots. We give her clean water, too.
A wild rabbit has a cozy hole in the ground. But for shelter, Miss Bunny
has a cage in our classroom's Quiet Corner.*

Confirming Understanding

Distribute crayons. Develop the science concept
by asking questions about the story. Ask:

• *Why does Miss Bunny get fresh hay and
vegetables?* (Animals need food.) *Use
orange to circle Miss Bunny's food.*

• *Why does Miss Bunny get clean water?*
(Animals need water.) *Make a blue dot on
the water.*

• *What is the rabbit cage for?* (shelter; a safe
place) *Draw a red line under the cage.*

• *What four things do animals need?*
(food, water, air, shelter)

Day 1 picture

Life Science

• Understand that plants, animals, and people are living things that have basic needs

Literacy

Oral Language Development

• Respond orally to simple questions

Comprehension

• Recall details

• Make connections using illustrations, prior knowledge, or real-life experiences

Reinforcing the Concept

Reread the Day 1 story. Then reinforce this week's science concept by guiding a discussion about the story. Say:

Our story named four things that animals need to live. What are they? (food, water, air, shelter)

Distribute the Day 2 activity and crayons. Say:

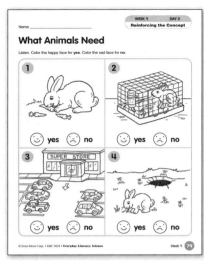

Day 2 activity

• *Point to box 1. Animals need food. Does this rabbit have food? Color the happy face for **yes** or the sad face for **no**.* (yes) *What kind of food is it?* (carrots, grass)

• *Point to box 2. Animals need shelter. Does this rabbit have shelter? Color the happy face for **yes** or the sad face for **no**.* (yes) *What is the rabbit's shelter?* (cage)

• *Point to box 3. Animals need food, water, air, and shelter. Is a parking lot a good place for a rabbit to live? Color the happy face for **yes** or the sad face for **no**.* (no) *Why?* (It is dangerous; There is no food, water, or shelter.)

• *Point to box 4. Is a hole in the ground a good place for a wild rabbit to live? Color the happy face for **yes** or the sad face for **no**.* (yes) *Why?* (It can hide in the hole to stay safe: It can come out to find food and water.)

Life Science

• Understand that plants, animals, and people are living things that have basic needs

Literacy

Oral Language Development

• Respond orally to simple questions

• Use new vocabulary

Comprehension

• Make connections using illustrations, prior knowledge, or real-life experiences

Developing the Concept

To introduce the activity, guide a discussion that helps students recall the Day 1 story. Say:

Our story was about a pet rabbit. A rabbit is a living thing that needs food, water, air, and shelter. Who took care of Miss Bunny and gave her the things she needed? (the class)

Distribute the Day 3 activity and crayons. Say:

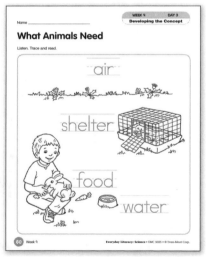

Day 3 activity

• *Look at the picture. Animals need air to breathe. Air is everywhere, but we cannot see it. Where is the air in this picture?* (everywhere) *Put your crayon on the word **air**. Trace the letters and read the word.*

• *Things that an animal needs have a name written by them. Point to the rabbit cage. What is a cage for?* (shelter) *Put your crayon on the word **shelter**. Trace the letters and read the word.*

• *Point to the carrot. What is a carrot for?* (food) *Put your crayon on the word **food**. Trace the letters and read the word.*

• *Point to the dish. What does the dish hold that animals need?* (water) *Put your crayon on the word **water**. Trace the letters and read the word.*

Life Science

• Understand that plants, animals, and people are living things that have basic needs

Literacy

Oral Language Development

• Name and describe pictured objects

• Use new vocabulary

Comprehension

• Recall details

Extending the Concept

Introduce the Day 4 activity by reviewing:

*People and animals are living things. They need food, water, air, and shelter. What is **shelter**?* (a place that is safe from weather and danger) *Let's see what kinds of shelter different animals live in.*

Distribute the Day 4 activity and crayons. Say:

• *Point to the first picture. What does it show?* (frog) *What is shelter for a frog?* (pond) *Draw a line from the frog to the picture of the pond.*

• *Point to picture 2. What does it show?* (baby birds) *What is shelter for baby birds?* (nest) *Draw a line from the baby birds to the nest.*

• *Point to picture 3. What does it show?* (a dog) *What is shelter for a dog?* (doghouse) *Draw a line from the dog to the doghouse.*

• *Point to picture 4. What does it show?* (a boy) *What is shelter for a boy?* (house) *Draw a line from the boy to the house.*

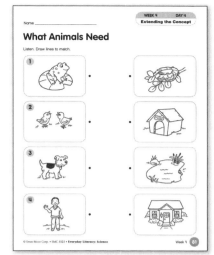

Day 4 activity

Life Science

• Understand that plants, animals, and people are living things that have basic needs

Literacy

Oral Language Development

• Use new vocabulary

Scientific Thinking & Inquiry

• Record observations and data with pictures and other symbols

Home–School Connection p. 82
Spanish version available (see p. 2)

Hands-on Science Activity

Reinforce this week's science concept with the following hands-on activity:

Materials: pictures of many kinds of animals, glue, drawing paper, sentence strip or lined sentence paper for each student

Preparation: Prepare a sentence strip for each student with an incomplete sentence that reads, **A _____ needs _____.**

Activity: Introduce the activity by saying:

You learned that animals are living things. What do animals need in order to live and grow? (food, water, air, shelter)

Display an animal picture and brainstorm the things the animal needs. For example, a horse needs water, a barn, and hay. A cat needs water, cat food, and a bed. Then have children complete their sentence strips with pictures or words. If they are able to complete the sentence with words, glue the sentence onto a sheet of construction paper and have them draw a picture of the animal below the sentence.

Name _____

What Animals Need

Everyday Literacy: Science • EMC 5025 • © Evan-Moor Corp.

Name _____

What Animals Need

Listen. Color the happy face for **yes**. Color the sad face for **no**.

Name _____

What Animals Need

Listen. Trace and read.

air

shelter

food

water

Everyday Literacy: Science • EMC 5025 • © Evan-Moor Corp.

Name _____

What Animals Need

Listen. Draw lines to match.

1    •   •

2    •   •

3    •   •

4    •   •

Name _____

What I Learned

What to Do

Have your child look at the picture below. Talk about the things that animals need to live and grow: food, water, air, and shelter. Have your child point to each one. Ask: *Which one cannot be seen?* (air) Then have your child color the picture.

Science Concept: Living things have basic needs.

To Parents
This week your child learned that animals need food, water, air, and shelter to live and grow.

Miss Bunny

What to Do Next

Help your child find and cut out a magazine picture of a pet and glue it onto drawing paper. Then have your child draw in details such as food, water, and a shelter for their pet.

Everyday Literacy: Science • EMC 5025 • © Evan-Moor Corp.

Concept
Living things can change and grow.

From Egg to Frog

Science Objective:
To help students understand that frogs are living things that change and grow—from egg to tadpole to adult

Science Vocabulary:
egg, frog, froglet, lungs, tadpole, tail

Day 1
SKILLS

Life Science
• Understand that people and animals are living things that grow and change

Literacy

Oral Language Development
• Respond orally to simple questions
• Use new vocabulary
• Use traditional structures, such as chronological order, to convey information

Comprehension
• Make connections using illustrations, prior knowledge, or real-life experiences
• Answer questions about key details in a text read aloud
• Make inferences and draw conclusions

Introducing the Concept

Distribute the Day 1 activity page. Then point to the frog. Say:

• *Have you ever seen a real frog? Have you ever touched one? What did it feel like?* (students respond)

• *Have you ever heard a frog? Make a sound like a frog.* (students respond)

• *Is a frog a living thing?* (yes) *Tell me what else you know about frogs.* (students respond)

Listening to the Story

Redirect students' attention to the Day 1 page. Say: *Listen and look at the picture as I read a story about a girl who learns about frogs.*

Last night I heard frogs croaking by the river. Where did all those frogs come from? Mom read me a book about frogs. It said that frogs start out as tiny eggs. The mother frog lays her eggs in water. Soon, babies called tadpoles push out of the eggs. Tadpoles have a tail but no legs. They can breathe underwater, but not on land. Tadpoles eat plants in the water. They begin to grow. First they grow back legs, then front legs. Their tail gets shorter and they turn into froglets. Inside their body, lungs grow so they can breathe on land. Before long, the froglets have changed into frogs. That's when you can hear them say, "Croak, croak, croak."

Confirming Understanding

Distribute crayons. Reinforce the science concept by asking questions about the story. Ask:

• *Where does a mother frog lay her eggs?* (in water) *Circle the frog eggs.*

• *What pushes out of a frog egg?* (tadpole) *Does it have a tail?* (yes) *Does it have legs?* (no) *Draw a brown line under the tadpole.*

• *What does a tadpole grow?* (legs, lungs) *Draw a green line under the froglet.*

• *What does the froglet become?* (frog) *Can a frog breathe on land?* (yes) *Color the frog green.*

Day 1 picture

Day 2
SKILLS

Life Science
• Understand that people and animals are living things that grow and change

Literacy

Oral Language Development
• Respond orally to simple questions
• Use new vocabulary

Comprehension
• Recall details
• Make connections using illustrations, prior knowledge, or real-life experiences
• Make inferences and draw conclusions

Reinforcing the Concept

Reread the Day 1 story. Then reinforce this week's science concept by guiding a discussion about the story. Say:

Our story told how tadpoles change into frogs. What is a baby frog called? (tadpole)

Distribute the Day 2 activity and crayons. Say:

• *Point to box 1. Mother frogs lay their eggs in water. Are these frog eggs in water? Color the happy face for **yes** or the sad face for **no**.* (yes) *Point to the eggs.*

• *Now point to box 2. A tadpole has a tail but no legs. Does this tadpole have legs? Color the happy face for **yes** or the sad face for **no**.* (no) *What does it have?* (a tail)

• *Now point to box 3. As a tadpole grows, it becomes a froglet. Its tail gets shorter. It grows legs. Does this froglet have legs? Color the happy face for **yes** or the sad face for **no**.* (yes) *How many legs are there?* (four)

• *Point to box 4. Does this picture show a tadpole? Color the happy face for **yes** or the sad face for **no**.* (no) *What is this?* (a frog)

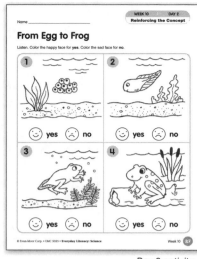

Day 2 activity

Day 3
SKILLS

Life Science
• Understand that people and animals are living things that grow and change

Literacy

Oral Language Development
• Respond orally to simple questions
• Use new vocabulary

Comprehension
• Make connections using illustrations, prior knowledge, or real-life experiences

Applying the Concept

To introduce the activity, guide a discussion that helps children recall the Day 1 story. Say:

In our story, a girl and her mom read a book about frogs. How does a frog grow? (starts as an egg, then becomes a tadpole, then a froglet, then a frog)

Distribute the Day 3 activity and pencils. Say:

• *These pictures show how a frog grows. What does picture 1 show?* (frog eggs) *This picture has the word **eggs** under it. Put your pencil on the word **eggs**. Trace the letters and then read the word to me.*

• *What does picture 2 show?* (a tadpole) *A tadpole has a tail and no legs. Put your pencil on the word **tadpole**. Trace the letters and then read the word to me.*

• *Look at picture 3. What does it show?* (a froglet) *A froglet has legs in front and back. Its tail gets shorter, too. Put your pencil on the word **froglet**. Trace the letters and then read the word to me.*

• *Look at picture 4. What does it show?* (a frog) *Does a frog have a tail?* (no) *Does a frog have legs?* (yes) *Put your pencil on the word **frog**. Trace the letters and then read the word to me.*

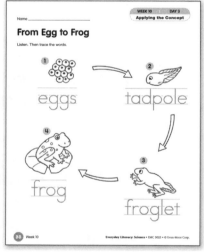

Day 3 activity

Day 4
SKILLS

Life Science
• Understand that people and animals are living things that grow and change

Literacy

Oral Language Development
• Respond orally to simple questions
• Use new vocabulary

Comprehension
• Recall details
• Make connections using illustrations, prior knowledge, or real-life experience

Applying the Concept

Distribute the Day 4 activity and crayons. Say:

A tadpole hatches from an egg. Then it grows into a froglet, then a frog. These pictures show the stages of a frog's life.

- *A mother frog laid her eggs in water. Which picture shows frog eggs? Draw a line from that picture to number 1.*

- *One day a tadpole pushed out of its egg. It had a flat tail. It had no legs. Which picture shows the tadpole? (tadpole with no legs) Draw a line from that picture to number 2.*

- *The tadpole grew and grew. It grew legs. Its tail became shorter. It became a froglet. Which picture shows the froglet? (froglet with legs) Draw a line from that picture to number 3.*

- *What happened last? (It became a frog.) Draw a line from that picture to number 4.*

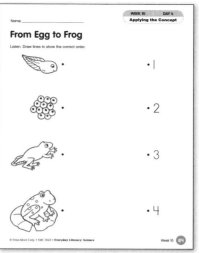

Day 4 activity

Day 5
SKILLS

Life Science
• Understand that people and animals are living things that grow and change

Literacy

Oral Language Development
• Use new vocabulary

Scientific Thinking & Inquiry
• Record observations and data with pictures and other symbols

Home–School Connection p. 90
Spanish version available (see p. 2)

Hands-on Science Activity

Reinforce this week's science concept with the following hands-on activity:

Materials: drawing paper, crayons, scissors, and glue sticks; paper or self-adhesive labels to make word list

Preparation: Divide a sheet of paper into fourths. In each section, write or type this word list: **eggs, tadpole, froglet, frog.** Make enough photocopies so each student has a set of four words to cut apart. (Self-adhesive address labels would work as well.)

Activity: Distribute the drawing paper and have students fold it twice to make four sections. Explain that they will make a drawing in each box and stick on a word that labels it. Help them number the boxes **1, 2, 3,** and **4.** Then say:

- *Draw some frog eggs in box 1.*

- *Draw a tadpole in box 2. Make a tail but no legs.*

- *Draw a froglet in box 3. Make legs and a short tail.*

- *Draw a frog in box 4.*

- *Cut apart your words. Glue one word in each box to name the pictures.*

Name _____

From Egg to Frog

Everyday Literacy: Science • EMC 5025 • © Evan-Moor Corp.

Name _____

From Egg to Frog

Listen. Color the happy face for **yes**. Color the sad face for **no**.

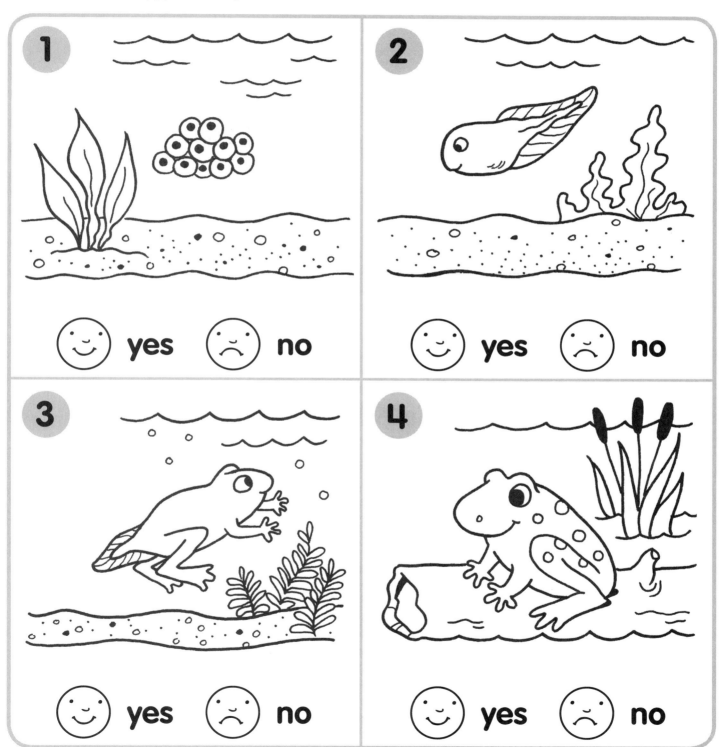

Name _____

From Egg to Frog

Listen. Then trace the words.

1 eggs

2 tadpole

3 froglet

4 frog

Name _____

From Egg to Frog

Listen. Draw lines to show the correct order.

   •   • 1

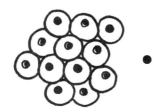   •   • 2

   •   • 3

   •   • 4

Name _____

What I Learned

What to Do
Have your child look at the picture below and point to the frog eggs, tadpole, froglet, and frog. Then discuss the changes that happen as a frog grows: a tadpole pushes out of an egg; a tadpole has no legs, only a tail; a froglet grows legs and its tail gets shorter; and finally it is a frog.

Science Concept: Living things can change and grow.

To Parents
This week your child learned that a tadpole hatches from an egg, grows, and changes into a frog.

What to Do Next
Take a discovery walk with your child. Look for animals of various sizes and types. Together, make a list of the animals you see.

Everyday Literacy: Science • EMC 5025 • © Evan-Moor Corp.

I'm Growing!

Science Objective:
To help students understand that they are living things that change and grow

Science Vocabulary:
adult, baby, grow, inches, learn, measure, teenager, teeth

Day 1 SKILLS

Life Science
• Understand that people and animals are living things that grow and change

Literacy

Oral Language Development
• Respond orally to simple questions

Comprehension
• Make connections using illustrations, prior knowledge, or real-life experiences
• Answer questions about key details in a text read aloud
• Make inferences and draw conclusions

Introducing the Concept

Begin by activating students' prior knowledge about how they grow. Say:

• *Are you growing? How do you know?* (clothes get small; I look different)

• *As you grow, your body gets bigger. As you grow, you can do more things, too. You might learn to do something you couldn't do before.*

• *Today, let's measure to see how tall you are.*

Then measure and record each student's height on a strip of paper (use calculator tape or butcher paper). Save the paper and repeat the activity at the end of the year so each student can see his or her growth.

Listening to the Story

Distribute the Day 1 activity page. Say: *Listen and look at the pictures as I read a story about a girl who is growing.*

My name is Mia. In school, I learned that living things grow and change. A long time ago, I was a baby. Now I am five years old and I have grown. When I was a baby, I didn't have teeth. Now I have all my teeth. When I was a baby, someone had to carry me. Then I learned to crawl. When I first learned to walk, I fell down a lot. Now I walk, run, and even ride a bike. My mom says I was 20 inches long when I was born. Now I am 40 inches tall. I'm growing!

Confirming Understanding

Distribute crayons. Develop the science concept by asking questions about the story. Ask:

• *What does Mia have now that she didn't have when she was a baby?* (teeth) *Circle Mia's teeth.*

• *Does Mia move differently now than she did when she was a baby?* (yes) *Which picture shows how Mia can move now?* (Mia running) *Circle Mia running.*

• *Find the picture that shows how tall Mia was when she was a baby. Draw a line above Mia's head in the picture that shows how tall she is now.*

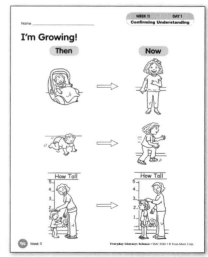

Day 1 picture

Life Science
- Understand that people and animals are living things that grow and change

Literacy

Oral Language Development
- Respond orally to simple questions

Comprehension
- Recall details
- Make connections using illustrations, prior knowledge, or real-life experiences

Reinforcing the Concept

Reread the Day 1 story. Then reinforce this week's science concept by guiding a discussion about the story. Say:

Our story tells us about a girl who is growing. What things can a kindergartner do that a baby cannot do? (walk, run, ride a bike, etc.)

Distribute the Day 2 activity and crayons. Say:

- *Point to box 1. What do you see?* (a baby and a girl) *Do both of them have teeth? Color the happy face for* **yes** *or the sad face for* **no**. (no)

- *Point to box 2. Is the girl taller than the baby? Color the happy face for* **yes** *or the sad face for* **no**. (yes)

- *Point to box 3. Can the baby and the girl each ride a bike? Color the happy face for* **yes** *or the sad face for* **no**. (no)

- *Point to box 4. Do both the girl and the baby need to be carried? Color the happy face for* **yes** *or the sad face for* **no**. (no)

Day 2 activity

Life Science
- Understand that people and animals are living things that grow and change

Literacy

Oral Language Development
- Name and describe pictured objects
- Respond orally to simple questions

Comprehension
- Make connections using illustrations, prior knowledge, or real-life experiences
- Make inferences and draw conclusions

Developing the Concept

To introduce the activity, guide a discussion that helps children recall the Day 1 story. Say:

Mia is five years old. What did she find out when her mom measured her? (She is growing taller; She is 40 inches tall.)

Distribute the Day 3 activity and crayons. Say:

- *Point to the first picture. What does it show?* (baby crawling) *Mia crawled when she was a baby. What does she do now?* (walks) *Draw a line from the crawling baby to Mia walking.*

- *Point to picture 2. Is the baby big or small?* (small) *Mia gets taller as she gets older. Draw a line from the picture of baby Mia to the picture that shows how tall she is now.*

- *Point to picture 3. What is the baby doing?* (drinking a bottle) *What does Mia eat with now?* (eats with a dish and spoon) *Draw a line from the baby to Mia eating now.*

- *Point to picture 4. What toy does a baby play with?* (rattle) *What does Mia play with now?* (baseball bat) *Draw a line from the baby with a rattle to Mia playing with a baseball bat.*

Day 3 activity

Everyday Literacy: Science • EMC 5025 • © Evan-Moor Corp.

Life Science

- Understand that people and animals are living things that grow and change

Literacy

Oral Language Development

- Name and describe pictured objects
- Respond orally to simple questions

Comprehension

- Recall details
- Make connections using illustrations, prior knowledge, or real-life experiences
- Make inferences and draw conclusions

Applying the Concept

Introduce the activity by saying:

People are living things. Just like every other living thing, people grow and change.

- *Babies grow into children.*
- *Children grow into teenagers.*
- *Teenagers become grown-ups, or adults.*

Distribute the Day 4 activity and crayons. Say:

- *This page shows a boy named Cole. When Cole was born, he was small. He could do three things very well—sleep, eat, and cry when he needed something. Which picture shows Cole soon after he was born?* (the baby in the crib) *Draw a line from that picture to number 1.*
- *Cole grew, and when he was five he went to kindergarten. Which picture shows Cole when he was five?* (a boy getting on a school bus) *Draw a line from the picture to number 2.*
- *Every year, Cole grew more and more. He learned how to do new things. Which picture shows Cole doing something he couldn't do when he was a boy?* (a teenager driving a car) *Draw a line from the picture to number 3.*
- *Cole grew up. He wasn't a teenager anymore. Which picture shows Cole as an adult?* (a man) *Draw a line from the picture to number 4.*

Day 4 activity

Life Science

- Understand that people and animals are living things that grow and change

Literacy

Oral Language Development

- Use traditional structures, such as chronological order, to convey information

Scientific Thinking & Inquiry

- Sort objects according to common characteristics

Home–School Connection p. 98
Spanish version available (see p. 2)

Hands-on Science Activity

Reinforce this week's science concept with the following hands-on activity:

Materials: magazines, bulletin board paper, glue, scissors

Preparation: Post the bulletin board paper lengthwise at a height that students can reach.

Activity: Create a picture timeline that shows people at different ages or stages of growth. Have students find magazine pictures of people of different ages engaged in different activities. Each student should find 3 to 5 pictures and cut them out. Then help the students group the pictures and glue them onto the timeline from youngest to oldest. Ask for pictures of babies first, then school-age children, teenagers, and grown-ups. Guide the sorting by asking questions, such as:

- *What things can a baby do?*
- *What things can children do?*
- *What things can teenagers do?*
- *What things can grown-ups do?*

Name _____

I'm Growing!

Then

Now

 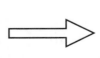

Everyday Literacy: Science • EMC 5025 • © Evan-Moor Corp.

Name _____

I'm Growing!

Listen. Color the happy face for **yes**. Color the sad face for **no**.

Name _____

I'm Growing!

Listen. Draw a line to match **then** and **now**.

 •

•

 •

•

 •

•

 •

•

Name _____

I'm Growing!

Listen. Draw lines to show the correct order.

 1

 2

3

4

Name _____

What I Learned

What to Do

Have your child look at the pictures below. Ask your child to tell you what is happening in each picture. Ask: *What are some ways that people grow or change?* Have your child number the pictures in the correct order. Then have your child color the pictures.

WEEK 11
Home–School Connection

Science Concept: Living things can change and grow.

To Parents
This week your child learned that people are living things that change and grow.

What to Do Next

Look at your child's baby pictures together. Compare *then* and *now*. Talk about ways your child has grown.

Concept
Living things have parts.

Animals Have Parts

Science Objective:
To help students understand that animals are living things that have parts

Science Vocabulary:
beak, claws, feathers, fur, legs, scales, trunk, webbed

Day 1 SKILLS

Life Science
• Understand that animals, plants, and people are living things that have parts

Literacy

Oral Language Development
• Respond orally to simple questions

Comprehension
• Recall details
• Make connections using illustrations, prior knowledge, or real-life experiences
• Answer questions about key details in a text read aloud
• Make inferences and draw conclusions

Introducing the Concept

Introduce students to the concept that different animals have different body parts and outer coverings. Say:

• *Animals are living things. Living things grow and change. Animals have body parts that help them live. Some animals have fur to keep them warm. Do you know of any animals with fur?* (students respond)

• *Some animals have feathers to keep them warm and to help them fly. What animals with feathers have you seen?* (birds, ducks)

• *Some animals have scales. Scales protect an animal's skin from water or rough ground. What animal has scales?* (snake, fish, lizard, etc.)

• *Some animals have feet that help them do different things. How does an animal use its feet?* (to run, climb, swim, etc.)

Listening to the Story

Distribute the Day 1 activity page. Say: *Listen and look at the picture as I read a story about a boy at the zoo.*

At the zoo, Jake saw all kinds of animals. He saw a bear with thick fur that kept it warm. It walked on four legs and had sharp claws for climbing. Jake saw a crocodile covered with scales. It used its tail and webbed feet to zoom through the water. And its four legs made it fast on land, too. By the pond, Jake saw a duck. It had feathers to keep it warm and to help it fly. Splash! The duck flew into the pond and swam away, paddling with its webbed feet.

Confirming Understanding

Distribute crayons. Reinforce the science concept by asking questions about the story. Ask:

• *Which animal had fur?* (bear) *Make a black dot on the bear's fur.*

• *Which animal had scales?* (crocodile) *Make an X on the crocodile.*

• *Which animal had feathers?* (duck) *Color a duck yellow.*

• *Which animals had webbed feet?* (duck, crocodile) *Circle the feet on both animals.*

Day 1 picture

Day 2
SKILLS

Life Science
• Understand that animals, plants, and people are living things that have parts

Literacy

Oral Language Development
• Name and describe pictured objects
• Respond orally to simple questions

Comprehension
• Recall details
• Make connections using illustrations, prior knowledge, or real-life experiences
• Answer questions about key details in a text read aloud
• Make inferences and draw conclusions

Reinforcing the Concept

Reread the Day 1 story. Then reinforce this week's science concept by guiding a discussion about the story. Say:

Our story tells about different kinds of animals.

> • *Name some of the different parts that animals have.* (fur, scales, feathers, tail, legs, feet, claws)

Distribute the Day 2 activity and crayons. Say:

> • *Point to box 1. Name these two animals that Jake saw at the zoo.* (duck, bear) *Do they both have fur to keep warm? Color the happy face for **yes** or the sad face for **no**.* (no) *Which one has fur?* (bear) *What covers the duck's body?* (feathers)

> • *Point to box 2. Name these two animals.* (crocodile, bear) *Do they both have a long tail that is useful for swimming? Color the happy face for **yes** or the sad face for **no**.* (no) *Which one has a long tail?* (crocodile)

> • *Point to box 3. Name the animal in the picture.* (bear) *Does a bear have sharp claws for climbing? Color the happy face for **yes** or the sad face for **no**.* (yes) *What do you think this bear wants to reach?* (honey)

> • *Point to box 4. Name the animal in the picture.* (duck) *Does the duck have webbed feet? Color the happy face for **yes** or the sad face for **no**.* (yes) *How does a duck use its webbed feet?* (as paddles to swim)

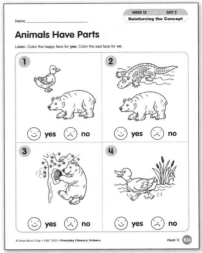

Day 2 activity

Day 3
SKILLS

Life Science
• Understand that animals, plants, and people are living things that have parts

Literacy

Oral Language Development
• Name and describe pictured objects
• Respond orally to simple questions

Comprehension
• Recall details
• Make connections using illustrations, prior knowledge, or real-life experiences

Applying the Concept

Distribute the Day 3 activity and crayons. Then introduce the activity by saying:

Some animals have feet and some do not. Animals use their feet in different ways. What are your feet useful for? (students respond)

> • *Now look at picture 1. How many webbed feet are there?* (two) *Which animal has two webbed feet?* (a duck) *How does it use them?* (to swim) *Find the picture of the duck's body. Draw a line from the feet to the duck.*

> • *Look at picture 2. What kind of feet do you see?* (big furry paws with claws) *Which animal has furry paws?* (bear) *How does it use its claws?* (to climb) *Draw a line to the bear.*

> • *Look at picture 3. What do you see?* (webbed feet with scales) *Which animal has scales and webbed feet?* (crocodile) *How does it use its feet?* (to move in water and on land) *Draw a line to the crocodile.*

> • *Look at picture 4. What do you see?* (two feet with five toes on each) *Who has feet like these?* (boy) *Draw a line to the boy.*

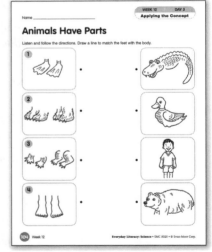

Day 3 activity

Life Science
- Understand that animals, plants, and people are living things that have parts

Literacy

Oral Language Development
- Name and describe pictured objects
- Respond orally to simple questions

Comprehension
- Recall details
- Make connections using illustrations, prior knowledge, or real-life experiences

Applying the Concept

Distribute the Day 4 activity and crayons. Then introduce the activity by saying:

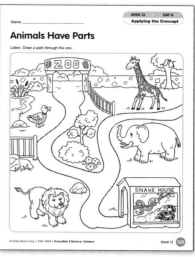

Day 4 activity

Animals have different parts for doing different things. At a zoo, you can watch how animals use their different parts.

- *This picture shows a zoo. Let's follow the path to see the animals.*

- *Put your crayon at the zoo entrance. Draw a line along the path to the animal with feathers. What animal is it?* (duck) *What other parts does a duck have?* (webbed feet, a beak, wings, etc.) *Circle the duck.*

- *The next animal we will see has fur covering its body. It has a big furry mane. What animal is it?* (lion) *Draw a line along the path from the duck to the lion. Color the lion's mane yellow.*

- *Now let's visit some animals that do <u>not</u> have legs. What animals are they?* (snakes) *Draw a line along the path from the lion to the snakes.*

- *Next, let's go see an animal with a very long nose called a trunk. What animal is it?* (elephant) *Draw a line along the path from the snake house to the elephant.*

- *Finally, let's go see an animal with a long neck. It can eat leaves from the treetops. What animal is it?* (giraffe) *Draw a line along the path from the elephant to the giraffe. Color the giraffe.*

Life Science
- Understand that animals, plants, and people are living things that have parts

Literacy

Oral Language Development
- Use new vocabulary

Scientific Thinking & Literacy
- Sort objects according to common characteristics

Home–School Connection p. 106
Spanish version available (see p. 2)

Hands-on Science Activity

Reinforce this week's science concept with the following hands-on activity:

Materials: chart paper, marker, glue stick; magazine pictures of animals having a variety of body coverings—fur, feathers, and scales

Preparation: Use the marker to divide the chart paper into three sections labeled **Fur**, **Feathers**, and **Scales**. Next to each label, attach a picture that gives an example of it.

Activity: Have students sort the magazine pictures and glue them onto the chart in the correct columns. Discuss each picture as it is placed. Have students name the animal and tell what kind of body covering it has.

Name _____

Animals Have Parts

Everyday Literacy: Science • EMC 5025 • © Evan-Moor Corp.

Name _____

Animals Have Parts

Listen. Color the happy face for **yes**. Color the sad face for **no**.

Name _____

Animals Have Parts

Listen and follow the directions. Draw a line to match the feet with the body.

1

•   •

2

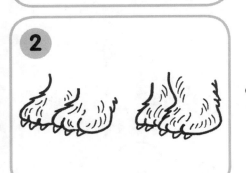

•   •

3

•   •

4

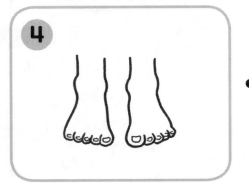

•   •

Name _____

Animals Have Parts

Listen. Draw a path through the zoo.

Name _____

What I Learned

What to Do

Have your child look at the picture below. Ask him or her to point to and name the zoo animals. Then have your child tell you some of the distinctive parts each animal has, for example: fur, feathers, scales, tail, webbed feet, long nose, long neck, and so on.

Science Concept: Living things have parts.

To Parents

This week your child learned that living things have different parts that do different things.

What to Do Next

Play "What Am I?" with your child. Give several clues about an animal, describing its parts. Have your child guess the animal. For example, say: *I have big paws. I have a long tail. I have a furry mane. What am I?* (lion)

Everyday Literacy: Science • EMC 5025 • © Evan-Moor Corp.

Concept
Plants have parts.

Trees Have Parts

Science Objective:
To help students understand that trees are plants and that plants have parts that help them live and grow

Science Vocabulary:
apple, blossoms, branches, leaves, roots, seeds, trunk

Day 1
SKILLS

Life Science
• Understand that animals, plants, and people are living things that have parts

Literacy

Oral Language Development
• Respond orally to simple questions
• Use new vocabulary

Comprehension
• Make connections using illustrations, prior knowledge, or real-life experiences
• Answer questions about key details in a text read aloud
• Make inferences and draw conclusions

Introducing the Concept

Begin by activating prior knowledge about different kinds of trees. Say:

• *Trees are plants. There are many different kinds of trees. Think about some trees you have seen. Do all trees look the same?* (no)

• *Trees have parts that help them live and grow. Can you name any of the parts of a tree?* (leaves, branches, trunk, roots)

• *Some trees grow fruit. Have you seen a tree that grows fruit?* (students respond) *What kind of fruit was growing?* (oranges, apples, pears, etc.)

Listening to the Story

Distribute the Day 1 activity page to each child. Say: *Listen and look at the picture as I read a story about a girl who learned about apple trees.*

Olivia's class went on a field trip to an apple farm. They saw rows of apple trees growing. The farmer told Olivia's class all about apple trees. He said that an apple tree has parts that help it grow and stay healthy. The roots take in water from the soil. The trunk carries the water up to the leaves. The leaves make food for the tree to help it grow. During the spring, flower blossoms grow on the tree. After the flowers are gone, the tree starts to grow apples. The apples are ready to pick in the fall. The farmer picked an apple and cut it open. He showed the children the seeds inside the apple. Guess what? If you plant the seeds, they grow into new apple trees!

Confirming Understanding

Distribute crayons or markers. Reinforce the science concept by asking students questions about the story. Say:

• *Name some parts of an apple tree.* (roots, trunk, leaves, blossoms, apple)

• *Which part takes water from the soil?* (roots) *Which part carries water to the leaves?* (trunk) *Color the roots and trunk brown.*

• *What fruit is growing on the trees?* (apples) *Color one apple red. What is inside an apple that can grow more apple trees?* (seeds) *Circle one apple seed.*

Day 1 picture

Life Science
- Understand that animals, plants, and people are living things that have parts

Literacy

Oral Language Development
- Respond orally to simple questions
- Use new vocabulary

Comprehension
- Recall details
- Make connections using illustrations, prior knowledge, or real-life experiences

Reinforcing the Concept

Reread the Day 1 story. Then reinforce this week's science concept by guiding a discussion about the story. Say:

> *Our story is about the parts of an apple tree. Which tree part makes food for the tree?* (leaves)

Distribute the Day 2 activity and crayons. Say:

- *Point to box 1. What kind of plant is this?* (tree) *Does the tree have roots? Color the happy face for* **yes** *or the sad face for* **no**. (yes) *Where are the roots?* (at the bottom; in the ground)

- *Now look at box 2. A tree trunk carries the water up to the leaves. The leaves make food for the tree. Does this tree have leaves? Color the happy face for* **yes** *or the sad face for* **no**. (no)

- *Look at box 3. What is growing on this tree?* (apples) *Do you pick apples and eat them? Color the happy face for* **yes** *or the sad face for* **no**. (yes)

- *Look at box 4. What do you see?* (halved apple; seeds) *Can apple seeds grow into new apple trees if you plant them? Color the happy face for* **yes** *or the sad face for* **no**. (yes)

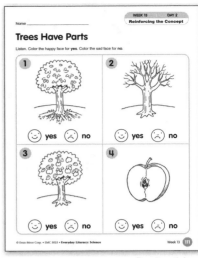

Day 2 activity

Life Science
- Understand that animals, plants, and people are living things that have parts

Literacy

Oral Language Development
- Respond orally to simple questions

Comprehension
- Make connections using illustrations, prior knowledge, or real-life experiences

Developing the Concept

Distribute the Day 3 activity and pencils. Then introduce the activity by saying:

> *The parts of a tree help it to live and grow. Let's label the parts of a tree.*

- *Point to the tree's roots. A tree has roots that hold it in the ground and take in water. Put your pencil on the word* **roots**. *Trace the letters. Now draw a line to the tree's roots.*

- *Point to the trunk. A tree has a trunk to carry water from the roots to the leaves. Put your pencil on the word* **trunk**. *Trace the letters. Then draw a line to the trunk.*

Day 3 activity

- *Point to the leaves. A tree has leaves to make food for the tree. Put your pencil on the word* **leaves**. *Trace the letters. Draw a line to one leaf.*

- *Point to the seed. Each tree grows a different kind of seed. Put your pencil on the word* **seed**. *Trace the letters. When you plant a seed, it grows into a new tree. If you plant a seed from an apple tree, what kind of tree will grow?* (an apple tree) *Draw a line to one seed.*

- *Now point to each word as I read it to you:* **roots, trunk, leaves, seed**.

Life Science

• Understand that animals, plants, and people are living things that have parts

Literacy

Comprehension

• Make connections using illustrations, prior knowledge, or real-life experiences

• Make inferences and draw conclusions

Applying the Concept

Distribute the Day 4 activity and crayons. Then introduce the activity by saying:

Trees are living things that grow and change.

Day 4 activity

• *Point to row 1. The first picture shows a tree. There are many different kinds of trees. Look at the rest of the pictures in this row. Circle the pictures that show trees.*

• *Point to row 2. The first picture shows a tree trunk. Trunks help carry the water to the leaves. Not all trunks look the same. Look at the rest of the pictures in this row. Circle the pictures that show tree trunks.*

• *Point to row 3. The first picture shows a leaf. Leaves make food for the tree. Not all leaves look the same. Look at the rest of the pictures in this row. Circle the pictures that show leaves.*

• *Point to row 4. The first picture shows roots. Roots help carry the water to the leaves. Look at the rest of the pictures in this row. Circle the pictures that show tree roots.*

Life Science

• Understand that animals, plants, and people are living things that have parts

Literacy

Oral Language Development

• Use new vocabulary

Scientific Thinking & Inquiry

• Record observations and data with pictures and other symbols

Home–School Connection p. 114
Spanish version available (see p. 2)

Hands-on Science Activity

Reinforce this week's science concept with the following hands-on activity:

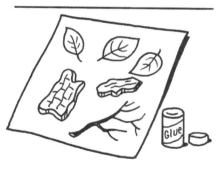

Materials: markers, glue; one sheet of construction paper and one lunch bag per child

Preparation: Write each student's name on a paper bag and a sheet of construction paper.

Activity: Distribute the paper bags to students. Explain that they will take a discovery walk around the school and collect tree parts. Tell them that they will use the tree parts they collect to make a *collage*, or a picture.

• Take students outside to look for leaves, bark, and other tree parts. Have students place what they collect in their bags.

• After you return to the classroom, distribute the labeled construction paper to each student.

• Have students glue their tree parts onto the construction paper to make a collage. Then have each student tell you what tree part the collected item is from. Help children label the items in their collage.

• Have students take turns telling the class about their tree-parts collage.

Trees Have Parts

Name _____

Trees Have Parts

Listen. Color the happy face for **yes**. Color the sad face for **no**.

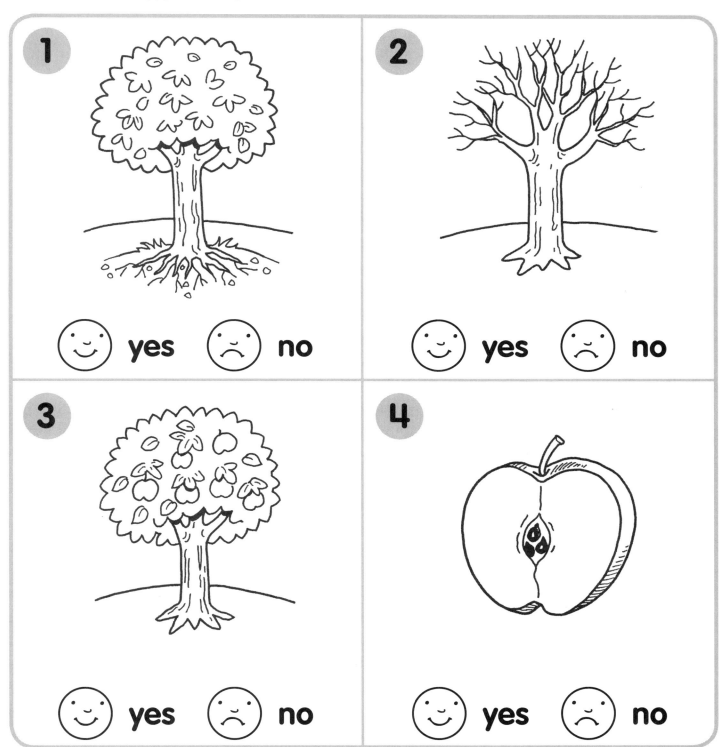

Name _____

Trees Have Parts

Listen. Follow the directions.

roots •

trunk •

leaves •

seed •

Everyday Literacy: Science • EMC 5025 • © Evan-Moor Corp.

Name _____

Trees Have Parts

Listen. Follow the directions.

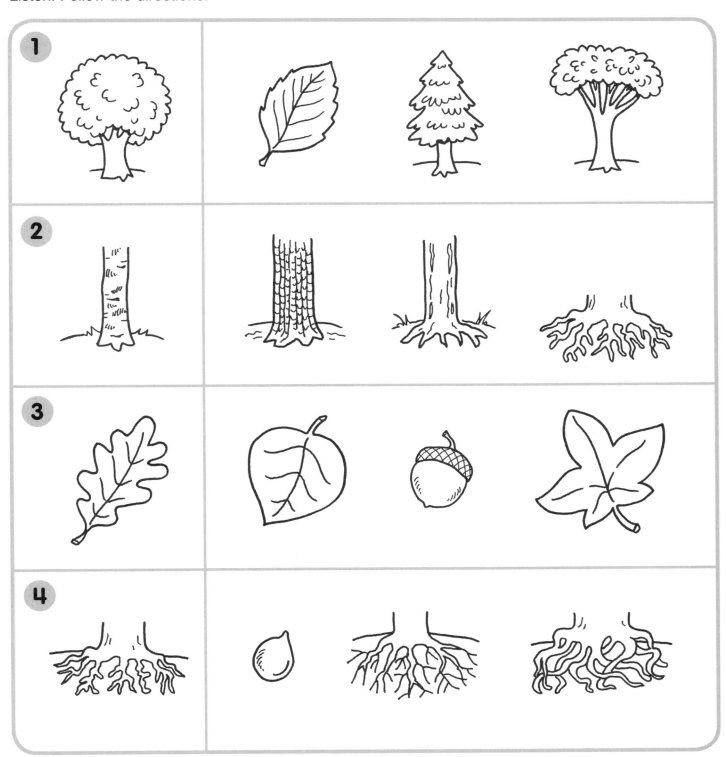

Name _____

What I Learned

What to Do
Have your child look at the picture and tell you where apples come from. Name these parts of an apple tree and have your child point to each one: *roots, trunk, leaves, apples.* Then ask your child to color the picture.

Science Concept: Plants have parts.

To Parents
This week your child learned that an apple tree is a plant with parts that help it live and grow.

What to Do Next
Have your child name foods made with apples while you write them in a list. Then have your child draw a picture of one of the foods.

WEEK 14

Concept
Living things
have parts.

My Body Has Parts

Science Objective:
To help students identify the parts of the body

Science Vocabulary:
ankles, arms, elbows, feet, fingers, hands, head, knees, legs, neck, toes, wrist

Day 1
SKILLS

Life Science
• Understand that animals, plants, and people are living things that have parts

Literacy

Oral Language Development
• Respond orally to simple questions
• Use new vocabulary

Comprehension
• Make connections using illustrations, prior knowledge, or real-life experiences
• Answer questions about key details in a text read aloud

Introducing the Concept

Activate students' prior knowledge about the parts of the human body. Say:

• *We use our body parts to play and have fun. We use our arms to throw a ball. We use our legs to run.*

• *How else do we use our body parts to play?* (students respond)

• *Each body part has a special job to do. Our bodies help us do many things.*

Listening to the Story

Distribute the Day 1 activity page. Say: *Listen and look at the picture as I read a story about a boy who uses his body parts at the beach.*

Aiden uses his body parts to have fun at the beach. Aiden turns his head to watch the waves crash on the shore. His neck holds his head up and helps it turn. Aiden uses his arms and hands to build a sand castle. His fingers bend and help him hold the shovel. Aiden's arms bend at his elbows, helping him lift a pail of sand. Aiden's legs help him run in the sand. He bends his legs at the knees and jumps over the sand castle. Then he lands on his feet. His toes help him balance. The beach is a great place to run, jump, and play!

Confirming Understanding

Distribute crayons. Reinforce the science concept by asking questions about the story. Say:

• *Look at the first picture. What body part holds up Aiden's head?* (neck) *Make an **X** on his neck in the first picture.*

• *Look at Aiden making a sand castle. What body part bends his arms?* (elbows) *Draw a circle around each elbow.*

• *Look at Aiden jumping. Where are his toes?* (on his feet) *Make an **X** on one toe.*

• *Point to each part in the last picture as I name it:* **head, neck, arms, elbows, hands, fingers, legs, knees, feet, ankles, toes**.

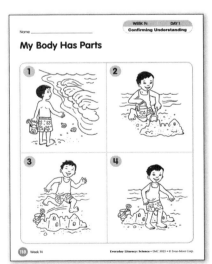

Day 1 picture

Life Science
- Understand that animals, plants, and people are living things that have parts

Literacy

Oral Language Development
- Name and describe pictured objects
- Respond orally to simple questions

Comprehension
- Make connections using illustrations, prior knowledge, or real-life experiences
- Answer questions about key details in a text read aloud

Reinforcing the Concept

Reread the Day 1 story. Then reinforce this week's science concept by guiding a discussion about the story. Say:

In our story, Aiden had fun at the beach. Which of his body parts did he use to make a sand castle? (all of them, but especially his arms and hands)

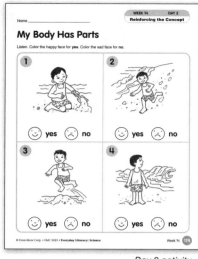

Day 2 activity

Distribute the Day 2 activity and crayons. Say:

- *Point to box 1. What is Aiden doing?* (holding a shovel) *Is he using his hands and fingers to hold it? Color the happy face for* **yes** *or the sad face for* **no**. (yes)

- *Point to box 2. What is Aiden doing?* (running) *Is he using his legs and feet to run? Color the happy face for* **yes** *or the sad face for* **no**. (yes)

- *Point to box 3. What is Aiden doing?* (jumping) *Is he using his neck to lift off the ground? Color the happy face for* **yes** *or the sad face for* **no**. (no) *What body parts is he mostly using?* (legs, knees, feet)

- *Point to box 4. What is Aiden doing?* (looking at the waves) *Is he bending his knees to do that? Color the happy face for* **yes** *or the sad face for* **no**. (no) *Which part helps him turn his head to look?* (neck)

Life Science
- Understand that animals, plants, and people are living things that have parts

Literacy

Oral Language Development
- Respond orally to simple questions
- Use new vocabulary

Comprehension
- Recall details
- Make connections using illustrations, prior knowledge, or real-life experiences

Developing the Concept

Distribute the Day 3 activity and crayons. Then introduce the activity by saying:

Your body has many parts. Each part has a job to do. Look at the picture of the boy. It shows many body parts.

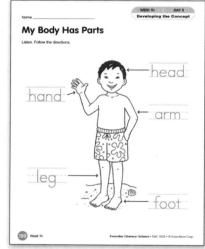

Day 3 activity

- *Point to the boy's head. What are some of its jobs?* (see, hear, smell, taste, smile, etc.) *Trace the word* **head**.

- *Point to the boy's hand. What can hands do?* (students respond) *Trace the word* **hand**.

- *Point to the boy's arm. What can arms do?* (students respond) *Trace the word* **arm**.

- *Point to the boy's leg. What can legs do?* (students respond) *Trace the word* **leg**.

- *Point to the boy's foot. What can feet do?* (students respond) *Trace the word* **foot**.

Have students work with a partner to point to and name other body parts in the picture, such as neck, wrist, finger, elbow, knee, ankle, and toe.

Life Science
• Understand that animals, plants, and people are living things that have parts

Literacy

Oral Language Development
• Respond orally to simple questions
• Use new vocabulary

Comprehension
• Make connections using illustrations, prior knowledge, or real-life experiences
• Respond appropriately to verbal commands

Extending the Concept

Review parts of the body by having students stand and follow your directions. Say:

Your body has many parts that can do many things. Show me how you can:

- *Touch your hands to your neck.*
- *Touch your elbows to your knees.*
- *Touch your finger to your nose.*
- *Touch your hands to your feet.*

Distribute the Day 4 activity and crayons. Say:

- *Point to number 1. Maria likes to throw a ball. Which picture shows the body parts she uses to throw?* (arm and hand) *Circle the picture of the arm and hand.*

- *Point to number 2. Aiden likes to kick a ball. Which picture shows the body parts he uses?* (leg and foot) *Circle the picture of the leg and foot.*

- *Point to number 3. Maria likes to play the drum. Which picture shows the body parts she uses?* (hands and fingers) *Circle the picture of the hands and fingers.*

- *Point to number 4. Aiden likes to march in time to the music. Which picture shows the body parts he uses?* (legs, knees, feet) *Circle the picture of the leg, knee, and foot.*

Day 4 activity

Life Science
• Understand that animals, plants, and people are living things that have parts

Literacy

Comprehension
• Respond appropriately to verbal commands

Home–School Connection p. 122
Spanish version available (see p. 2)

Hands-on Science Activity

Reinforce this week's science concept and vocabulary with the following hands-on activity:

Materials: masking tape or a ball of string; a large open space such as a playground

Preparation: Use the tape or string to make a large circle on the playground. Have students stand outside the circle.

Activity: Introduce the activity by saying:

People have many body parts. You know the names of many of those parts. Listen carefully. If I name a part you have, then you may step into the circle.

Name a physical feature (e.g., brown eyes, one nose, two elbows, red hair). Tell everyone in the class with that feature to step into the circle. Continue naming parts, with students moving in and out of the circle. Occasionally name a characteristic that no student possesses (e.g., three arms). End with a feature that everyone has.

Name _____

My Body Has Parts

Name _____

My Body Has Parts

Listen. Color the happy face for **yes**. Color the sad face for **no**.

My Body Has Parts

Listen. Follow the directions.

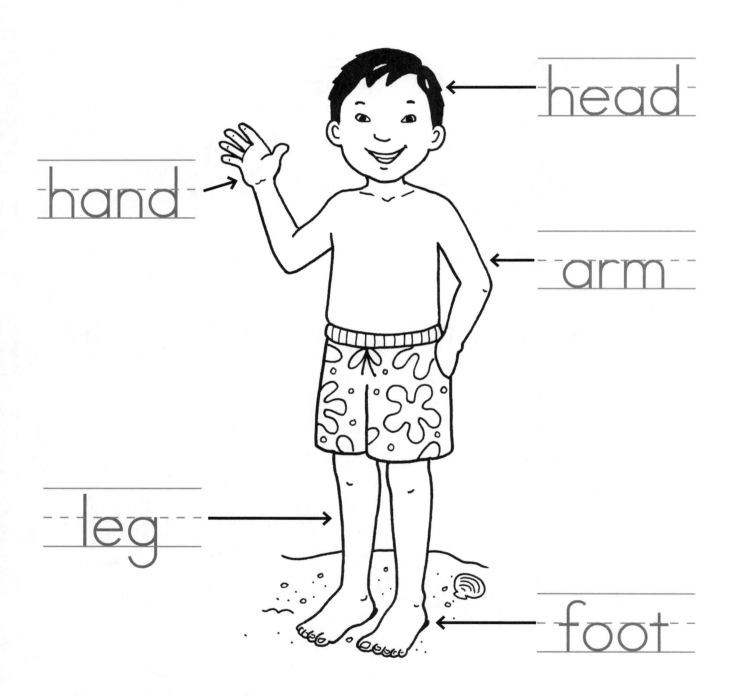

Name _____

My Body Has Parts

Listen. Follow the directions.

1 			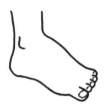
2 			
3 			
4 			

Name _____

What I Learned

What to Do
Have your child name each body part in the picture and then point to the same body part on his or her own body. Then have your child trace each word.

WEEK 14
Home–School Connection

Science Concept: Living things have parts.

To Parents
This week your child learned to identify parts of the body and what they do.

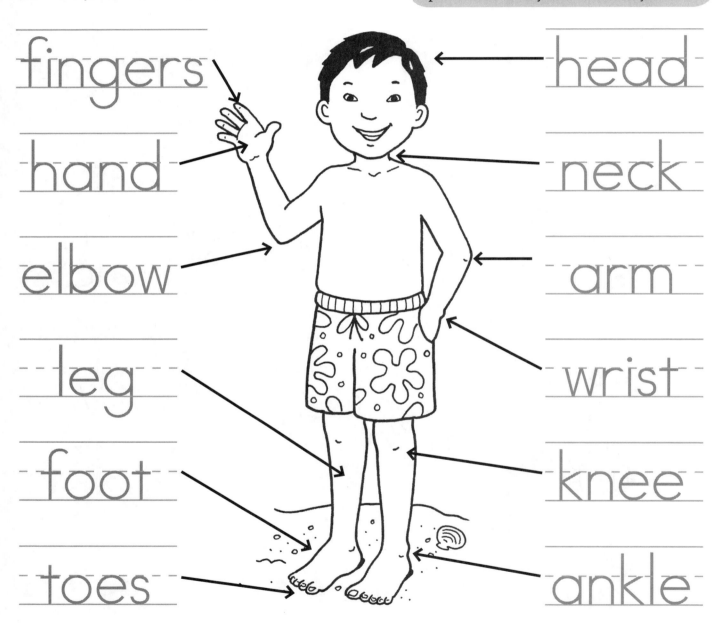

fingers

hand

elbow

leg

foot

toes

head

neck

arm

wrist

knee

ankle

What to Do Next
Play some dance music and challenge your child to follow directions. Say: *Dance with your head... dance with your elbows... dance with your fingers... dance on your toes,* and so on. Then have your child give you dance directions to follow.

WEEK 15

Concept
Earth has four seasons.

Four Seasons

Science Objective:
To help students understand that changes in weather occur from day to day and across seasons, affecting Earth and its people

Science Vocabulary:
fall, pattern, seasons, spring, summer, winter

Day 1 SKILLS

Earth Science
- Understand that the seasons change in a pattern
- Understand that there are different kinds of weather

Literacy

Oral Language Development
- Respond orally to simple questions

Comprehension
- Make connections using illustrations, prior knowledge, or real-life experiences
- Answer questions about key details in a text read aloud
- Make inferences and draw conclusions

Introducing the Concept

Begin by activating students' prior knowledge about the seasons. Ask:

- *Do we have the same weather every day?* (no) *How does the weather change?* (It may be sunny, cloudy, rainy, snowy, hot, warm, cold, etc.)
- *We have four seasons: spring, summer, fall, and winter. The weather often changes from season to season. What is the weather like in summer? fall? winter? spring?* (students respond)

Then introduce students to the concept of the patterns of the seasons. Say:

Our Earth is like a big ball that moves around the sun. As Earth moves, the seasons change from spring to summer to fall to winter.

Listening to the Story

Distribute the Day 1 activity page to each student. Say: *Listen and look at the picture as I read a story about the pattern of the seasons.*

In spring, the tree outside Ava's window has tiny, new green leaves. She hears baby birds chirping in their nest. Summer comes after spring. Now the tree has big, green leaves. Ava doesn't have school, so she sits in the shade of the tree and reads a book. Fall comes after summer. The leaves on the tree turn yellow, orange, and red before they fall to the ground. After school, Ava rakes up the leaves. Finally, winter comes. The branches of the tree are bare. One morning, Ava wakes up to see white snow covering everything! Ava likes the snow. But she knows that one day it will melt, spring will come, and the pattern will start all over again!

Confirming Understanding

Distribute crayons. Reinforce the science concept by asking questions about the story. Ask:

- *What does the tree have in spring?* (new green leaves) *Circle some of the leaves.*
- *What does the tree have in summer?* (big green leaves) *Color the tree's leaves.*
- *What does the tree have in fall?* (yellow, orange, red leaves) *Color the leaves on the ground red.*
- *In winter, the tree is bare. Circle the bare branches in black.*

Day 1 picture

Earth Science
- Understand that the seasons change in a pattern
- Understand that there are different kinds of weather

Literacy

Oral Language Development
- Name and describe pictured objects
- Respond orally to simple questions

Comprehension
- Make connections using illustrations, prior knowledge, or real-life experiences

Reinforcing the Concept

Reread the Day 1 story. Then reinforce this week's science concept by discussing the story. Say:

Our story tells us how the four seasons change. Name the seasons. (spring, summer, fall, winter)

Distribute the Day 2 activity and crayons. Say:

- *Point to row 1. In spring, Ava hears baby birds. The tree has tiny, new green leaves. Which picture in this row shows* **spring**? (the last picture) *Circle the last picture.*

- *Point to row 2. In summer, Ava reads under the tree. Its big green leaves give her shade. Which picture in this row shows* **summer**? (the first picture) *Circle the first picture.*

- *Point to row 3. In fall, Ava rakes up the yellow, orange, and red leaves that fall from the tree. Which picture in this row shows* **fall**? (the first picture) *Circle the first picture.*

- *Point to row 4. In winter, the tree branches are bare. Ava sees snow everywhere. Which picture in this row shows* **winter**? (the middle picture) *Circle the middle picture.*

Day 2 activity

Earth Science
- Understand that the seasons change in a pattern
- Understand that there are different kinds of weather

Literacy

Oral Language Development
- Name and describe pictured objects
- Respond orally to simple questions

Comprehension
- Make connections using illustrations, prior knowledge, or real-life experiences
- Make inferences and draw conclusions

Developing the Concept

Introduce the activity by saying:

The weather changes through the year as the seasons change. We wear different clothes to stay cool, warm, or dry in different seasons.

- *What do you wear to stay cool on a hot day? What do you wear to stay warm on a cold day?* (students respond)

Distribute the Day 3 activity and crayons. Say:

- *The pictures show the seasons. Let's number them to show the pattern. In spring it rains, so Joe wears a raincoat. Find the picture that shows Joe in the* **spring**. *Write the number* **1** *in the box. Joe is carrying a lunchbox and a backpack. Where do you think he might be going?* (to/from school)

Day 3 activity

- *Summer comes after spring. It is hot in the summer. Joe wears his swim trunks to stay cool. Find the picture that shows Joe in the* **summer**. *Write number* **2** *in the box. Where do you think Joe is?* (at the beach)

- *Fall comes after summer. On a cool fall day, Joe wears a sweater to stay warm. Find the picture that shows* **fall**. *Write number* **3** *in the box. What is Joe doing?* (raking leaves)

- *Winter comes after fall. Find the* **winter** *picture. Write number* **4**. *What is the weather like?* (cold, snowy) *What does Joe wear to stay warm?* (jacket, hat, scarf, mittens, boots) *What is he doing?* (building a snowman)

Day 4
SKILLS

Earth Science

• Understand that the seasons change in a pattern

• Understand that there are different kinds of weather

Literacy

Oral Language Development

• Name and describe pictured objects

• Respond orally to simple questions

• Use new vocabulary

Comprehension

• Make connections using illustrations, prior knowledge, or real-life experiences

Applying the Concept

Distribute the Day 4 activity and crayons. Say:

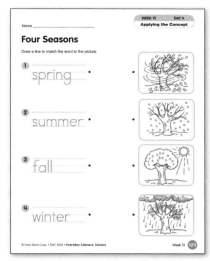

Day 4 activity

- *Point to number 1. This word is **spring**. Tiny new leaves grow on the trees in spring. The rainy weather helps plants grow. Which picture shows spring? (rainy day) Draw a line from the word **spring** to the picture of the rain falling on the tree. Now trace the word **spring**.*

- *Point to number 2. This word is **summer**. In summer, the sun shines and the weather is warm. Trees are full of green leaves. Which picture shows summer? (sunny day) Draw a line from the word **summer** to the picture of the sun shining onto a tree full of leaves. Now trace the word **summer**.*

- *Point to number 3. This word is **fall**. In fall, the weather is cool. The leaves fall off the trees and the wind blows them around. Which picture shows fall? (windy day) Draw a line from the word **fall** to the picture of the wind blowing the leaves. Now trace the word **fall**.*

- *Point to number 4. This word is **winter**. In winter, the weather is cold. Sometimes it is snowy. The tree branches are bare. Which picture shows winter? (snowy day) Draw a line from the word **winter** to the picture of snow falling onto the bare branches of a tree. Now trace the word **winter**.*

Day 5
SKILLS

Earth Science

• Understand that the seasons change in a pattern

• Understand that there are different kinds of weather

Scientific Thinking & Inquiry

• Record observations and data with pictures and other symbols

Home–School Connection p. 130
Spanish version available (see p. 2)

Hands-on Science Activity

Reinforce this week's science concept with the following hands-on activity:

Materials: one paper plate for each student; crayons or markers

Preparation: Using a black marker, divide each plate into four sections. Write the words **spring, summer, fall,** and **winter** around the edge of each plate.

Activity: Give each student a pre-labeled plate. Have them turn their plate slowly so they can see how the seasons occur in a cyclical pattern. Then guide students as they draw an icon to represent each season. Say:

> *The seasons change in a pattern. Let's start with spring. Rain helps plants grow in the spring. Draw raindrops under the word **spring**.*

Continue guiding students to draw an icon for each season: a sun for summer, a leaf for fall, and a snowman for winter. Then say:

> *The seasons follow a pattern. Point to each season as we name the pattern: **spring, summer, fall, winter**.*

Name _____

Four Seasons

Spring

Summer

Winter

Fall

Four Seasons

Listen and follow the directions. Circle the correct picture.

1

2

3

4

Name _____

Four Seasons

Number the pictures to show the pattern of the seasons.

Everyday Literacy: Science • EMC 5025 • © Evan-Moor Corp.

Name _____

Four Seasons

Draw a line to match the word to the picture.

1  •

2  •

3 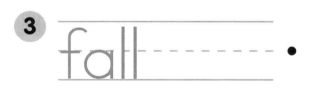 •

4  •

Name _____

What I Learned

What to Do

Have your child look at the pictures below. Ask him or her to
point to the pictures in order and name the seasons: spring,
summer, fall, winter. Ask: *Which season are we in now? Which
season do you like the most?* Have your child tell you an activity
he or she likes to do during each of the four seasons.

Science Concept: Earth has
four seasons.

To Parents
This week your child learned
that the Earth has four seasons.

Spring

Summer

Winter

Fall

What to Do Next

Help your child fold a sheet of drawing paper into four sections and draw a picture of what he or
she wears in each season.

Everyday Literacy: Science • EMC 5025 • © Evan-Moor Corp.

The Moon

Science Objective:
To help students understand that the moon is a big ball of rock that moves around the Earth

Science Vocabulary:
air, astronaut, crater, crescent, moon, phases, spacesuit, water

Introducing the Concept

Activate students' prior knowledge about the moon by saying:

The moon is an object in our sky. It is a big ball made of rock.

• *What is the biggest and brightest object you can see in the sky at night?* (the moon) *The moon looks bright because the sun shines on it and lights it up.*

• *Does the moon always look the same?* (No, sometimes it has a banana shape, sometimes it looks like a half circle, etc.)

Listening to the Story

Distribute the Day 1 activity page to each student. Say: *Listen and look at the pictures as I read a story about a girl who wonders about the moon.*

I wonder about the moon. My big brother Neil reads books about it. He says the moon looks small, but it isn't. The moon is a big ball of rock that is very far away. The moon looks smooth to me, but Neil says it isn't. The moon has big holes called craters. It has mountains and flat places, too. The moon looks like it changes shape, but Neil says it doesn't. The sun lights up the moon. Sometimes the sun doesn't shine on all of it, so we only see the part that is lit. Neil says the moon has a tiny bit of water, but no air. That's why plants, animals, and people can't live on the moon. After it gets dark, Neil and I are going outside to look up at the moon. I wonder what it will look like tonight!

Confirming Understanding

Distribute crayons or markers. Reinforce the science concept by asking students questions about the story. Ask:

• *Is the moon big or small?* (big) *Is it near or far away?* (far away) *Trace the moon.*

• *Is the moon smooth?* (No, it has holes, mountains, and flat places.) *What do we call the holes on the moon?* (craters) *Make an **X** on a moon crater.*

• *Are there plants and animals on the moon?* (no) *Why?* (no air; not enough water)

Day 1 picture

Earth Science

• Understand that the sun, moon, and stars are objects in our sky

• Explore properties of the moon and the stars

Literacy

Oral Language Development

• Respond orally to simple questions

Comprehension

• Make connections using illustrations, prior knowledge, or real-life experiences

• Recall details

Reinforcing the Concept

Reread the Day 1 story. Then reinforce this week's science concept by guiding a discussion about the story. Say:

Our story tells us about the moon. Tell me what you know about the moon. (It is a big ball of rock that is very far away, etc.)

Distribute the Day 2 activity and crayons. Say:

- *Point to box 1. Is the moon far from Earth? Color the happy face for **yes** or the sad face for **no**.* (yes)
- *Point to box 2. Is the moon smooth? Color the happy face for **yes** or the sad face for **no**.* (no) *Why not?* (It has craters, mountains, and flat places.)
- *Point to box 3. Do trees and other plants grow on the moon? Color the happy face for **yes** or the sad face for **no**.* (no) *Why not?* (There is no air on the moon.)
- *Point to box 4. Does the moon change shape? Color the happy face for **yes** or the sad face for **no**.* (no) *No, the moon doesn't change shape, it just looks like it does because we can only see the part of the moon that is lit by the sun.*

Day 2 activity

Earth Science

• Understand that the sun, moon, and stars are objects in our sky

• Explore properties of the moon and the stars

Literacy

Oral Language Development

• Respond orally to simple questions

Comprehension

• Recall details

• Make connections using illustrations, prior knowledge, or real-life experiences

Developing the Concept

Introduce the activity by reviewing the Day 1 story. Say:

People have visited the moon even though there is no air on the moon. These people are called astronauts, and they wear spacesuits that give them air to breathe.

Distribute the Day 3 activity and crayons. Say:

Pretend you are an astronaut. Let's draw a path to the things you see on the moon. Listen carefully and follow my directions.

- *First, put your crayon on the spaceship. You climb out of the spaceship in your spacesuit and see a moon crater. What is a crater?* (a big hole) *Draw a line from the spaceship to a crater.*
- *Second, you see rocks. The craters on the moon were made by rocks that crashed into the moon. The moon has many kinds of rocks. Draw a line from the crater to the rocks.*
- *Next, you see mountains. Draw a line from the rocks to the mountains.*
- *Last, you see footprints. Whose are they?* (student's; astronaut's) *Draw a line from the mountains to the footprints. Now get into your spaceship and fly home!*

Day 3 activity

Day 4
SKILLS

Earth Science
- Understand that the sun, moon, and stars are objects in our sky
- Explore properties of the moon and the stars

Literacy
Comprehension
- Make connections using illustrations, prior knowledge, or real-life experiences

Applying the Concept

Distribute the Day 4 activity and crayons. Then introduce the activity by saying:

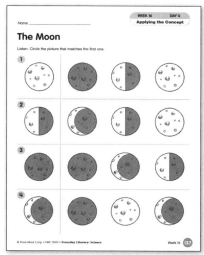

The moon looks small to us, but it is very big and far away. The moon moves around the Earth. The moon seems to change shape, but that is because we can only see the part of it that is lit up by the sun. What we see are the phases of the moon.

Day 4 activity

- *Point to row 1. Look at the first picture. It shows a full moon. The sun is shining on the part of the moon that we see. Circle the picture in this row that shows a full moon.*

- *Point to row 2. Look at the first picture. It shows a quarter moon. Only a part of the moon is lit up by the sun. Circle the picture in this row that shows a quarter moon.*

- *Point to row 3. Look at the first picture. It shows a dark moon. The moon is in the sky, but it is dark. We cannot see the part of it that is lit up by the sun. Circle the picture in this row that shows a dark moon.*

- *Point to row 4. Look at the first picture. It shows a crescent moon. This is the part of the moon that is lit up by the sun. Circle the picture in this row that shows a crescent moon.*

Day 5
SKILLS

Earth Science
- Understand that the sun, moon, and stars are objects in our sky
- Explore properties of the moon and the stars

Scientific Thinking & Inquiry
- Gather and record information through simple observations and investigations

Home–School Connection p. 138
Spanish version available (see p. 2)

Hands-on Science Activity

Reinforce this week's science concept with the following hands-on activity:

Materials: plastic dishpan, flour, yardstick, and four small balls of different weights, such as a golf ball, rubber ball, marble, or superball

Preparation: Fill the dishpan half full of flour and smooth it out. Say:

The moon has craters that were made by rocks that crashed into it long ago. Let's imagine that the flour in the dishpan is like the dusty surface of the moon, and these balls are rocks.

Activity: Have students place the balls in order by size. Then have them arrange the balls again by weight.

Hold the yardstick next to the dishpan and measure one foot high. Have students drop two balls from a height of one foot, and observe what happens. Remove the balls and compare the craters they made in the flour. Ask: *Which one went the deepest? Which one made the widest crater?* Smooth the flour and try two different balls. Compare the craters and record the observations. Then repeat this activity from a height of two feet and see what happens.

Name _____

The Moon

Name _____

The Moon

Listen. Color the happy face for **yes**. Color the sad face for **no**.

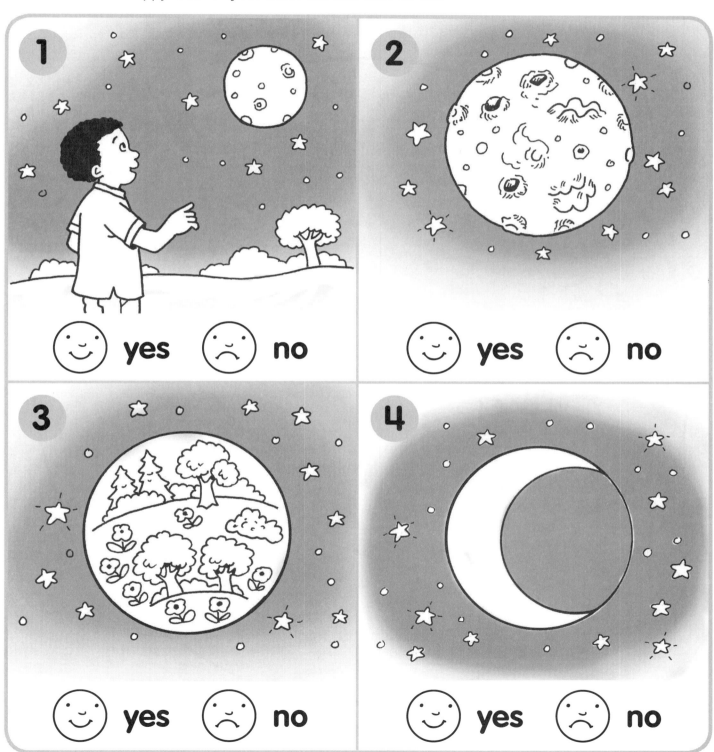

Name _____

The Moon

Listen. Follow the directions.

Name _____

The Moon

Listen. Circle the picture that matches the first one.

1

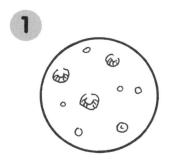 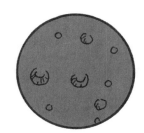 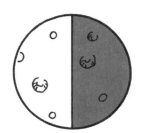 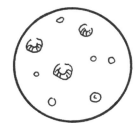

2

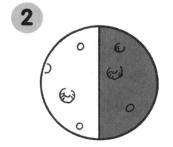 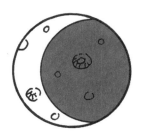 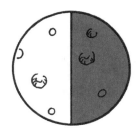 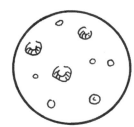

3

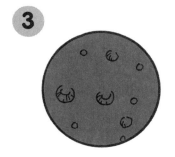 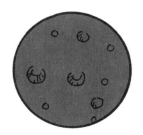 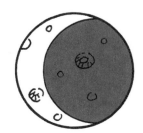 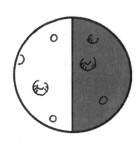

4

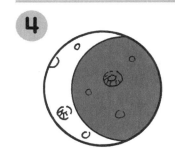 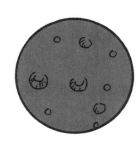 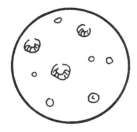 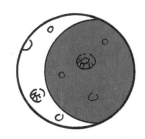

Name _____

What I Learned

What to Do
Have your child look at the picture below. Ask him or her to tell you what the children are doing. Have your child point to the moon and the stars. Then have your child color the picture.

Science Concept: The moon is an object in our sky.

To Parents
This week your child learned that the moon is an object in our sky.

What to Do Next
Go outside with your child and observe the moon. Then have your child draw a night scene that includes a picture of the same moon that you both just observed.

Everyday Literacy: Science • EMC 5025 • © Evan-Moor Corp.

Concept

The sun, moon, and stars are objects in our sky.

What Is a Star?

Science Objective:
To help students understand that a star is a ball of hot, glowing gas, and that stars form shapes (constellations) in the sky

Science Vocabulary:
Big Dipper, cloud, constellation, dust, gas, star, sun

Day 1 SKILLS

Earth Science
- Understand that the sun, moon, and stars are objects in our sky
- Explore properties of the moon and the stars

Literacy

Oral Language Development
- Respond orally to simple questions

Comprehension
- Make connections using illustrations, prior knowledge, or real-life experiences
- Answer questions about key details in a text read aloud

Introducing the Concept

Distribute the Day 1 activity page. Ask:

- *Have you ever looked up at the night sky? What did you see?* (e.g., moon, stars)

- *Do the stars look smaller or larger than the moon?* (smaller) *The stars look smaller than the moon, but in fact, they are much larger. They only look smaller because they are so far away from us. The moon is a lot closer to us than the stars, so it looks larger.*

- *Stars light up the sky because they are giant balls of hot, glowing gas. They give off light. Our sun is a star, too.*

Listening to the Story

Redirect students' attention to the Day 1 page. Say: *Listen and look at the picture as I read a story about a boy who watches the stars.*

I like to watch the stars at night. My brother told me that a star is a giant ball of hot, glowing gas. He said that our sun is a star. It looks bigger than the other stars because it is the closest star to Earth. The sun is so bright that we can't see the other stars during the day. But at night we can see hundreds of stars in the sky. Some of the stars make patterns in the sky. My brother and I thought we saw a group of stars that looked like a triangle. What do you see?

Confirming Understanding

Distribute crayons. Reinforce the science concept by asking questions about the story. Ask:

- *What is a star?* (a giant ball of hot, glowing gas) *Circle one star. What star is closest to Earth?* (the sun)

- *When can you see the stars?* (at night) *What else can you see in the night sky?* (the moon) *Color the moon yellow.*

- *Sometimes you can see patterns of stars in the night sky. Can you find your own star pattern in the picture? Draw lines to connect the stars and make a shape.*

Day 1 picture

Earth Science

- Understand that the sun, moon, and stars are objects in our sky
- Explore properties of the moon and the stars

Literacy

Oral Language Development

- Name and describe pictured objects
- Respond orally to simple questions

Comprehension

- Recall details
- Make connections using illustrations, prior knowledge, or real-life experiences

Reinforcing the Concept

Reread the Day 1 story. Then reinforce this week's science concept by activating students' prior knowledge. Say:

- *Stars are balls of hot, glowing gas. They are always giving off light, but we can't always see the light. When* **can** *we see the stars?* (at night)
- *What star can we see during the day?* (the sun)

Distribute the Day 2 activity and crayons. Say:

- *Point to box 1. Our sun is a star. Does this picture show a star? Color the happy face for* **yes** *or the sad face for* **no**. (yes)
- *Point to box 2. What does this picture show?* (the moon) *Is the moon a star? Color the happy face for* **yes** *or the sad face for* **no**. (no) *That's right, the moon is a ball of rock, not gas.*
- *Point to box 3. Does this picture show daytime or nighttime?* (nighttime) *What do you see in the sky?* (stars) *Could you see the stars if the picture showed daytime? Color the happy face for* **yes** *or the sad face for* **no**. (no)
- *Point to box 4. What does this picture show?* (the sun) *Is the sun the closest star to Earth? Color the happy face for* **yes** *or the sad face for* **no**. (yes)

Day 2 activity

Earth Science

- Understand that the sun, moon, and stars are objects in our sky
- Explore properties of the moon and the stars

Literacy

Oral Language Development

- Respond orally to simple questions

Comprehension

- Recall details
- Make connections using illustrations, prior knowledge, or real-life experiences

Applying the Concept

Introduce the activity by saying:

We are learning about the stars. Long ago, people thought certain groups of stars made shapes in the night sky. These groups were called **constellations**. *Some constellations were named after animals, and some were named after objects that people use every day.*

Distribute the Day 3 activity and crayons. Say:

- *The picture shows seven stars. Long ago, people named these seven stars the Big Dipper. The people thought the stars formed the shape of a ladle, or a big spoon that you dip into a pot. Point to each star and count with me: 1, 2, 3, 4, 5, 6, 7.*
- *Put your crayon on star number 1. Draw a line to star number 2. Then draw a line to star 3. Keep drawing to 4, 5, 6, and 7, to see the shape of the Big Dipper.*
- *Now look at the rest of the picture. Do you like to look at stars? Finish the picture to look like yourself!*

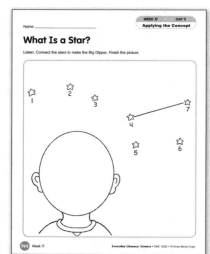

Day 3 activity

Applying the Concept

Introduce the activity by reviewing. Say:

Our sun is a star. It is made of hot, glowing gas. It is closer to us than all the other stars.

Distribute the Day 4 activity, pencils, and crayons. Say:

- *The picture on this page shows our sun. Look at number 1. The word is **sun**. Put your pencil on the word **sun**. Trace the letters and then read the word to me.* (sun)

- *Look at number 2. The word is **star**. Put your pencil on the word **star**. Trace the letters and then read the word to me.* (star)

- *Look at the sentence. It says, **Our sun is a star.** Read it with me.* (students respond) *Trace the words **sun** and **star** to finish the sentence.*

- *Color the sun to look like a giant ball of hot, glowing gas.*

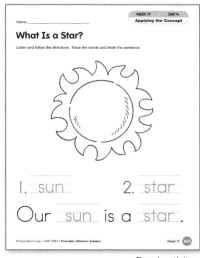

Day 4 activity

Hands-on Science Activity

Reinforce this week's science concept with the following hands-on activity:

Materials: drawing or photo of the Big Dipper; sheet of black construction paper, white chalk, and seven silver stick-on stars per child

Preparation: Write the words **Big Dipper** on the board where students can read it.

Activity: Direct students to use their seven stars to make the Big Dipper on their black paper. Show them a picture of the Big Dipper and say:

- *Make the Big Dipper with three stars for the long handle, and four stars for the cup.*

- *Use your piece of chalk to write the name **Big Dipper** on your paper.*

- *Now use your chalk to make dots for more stars around the Big Dipper.*

Name _____

What Is a Star?

Name _____

What Is a Star?

Listen. Color the happy face for **yes**. Color the sad face for **no**.

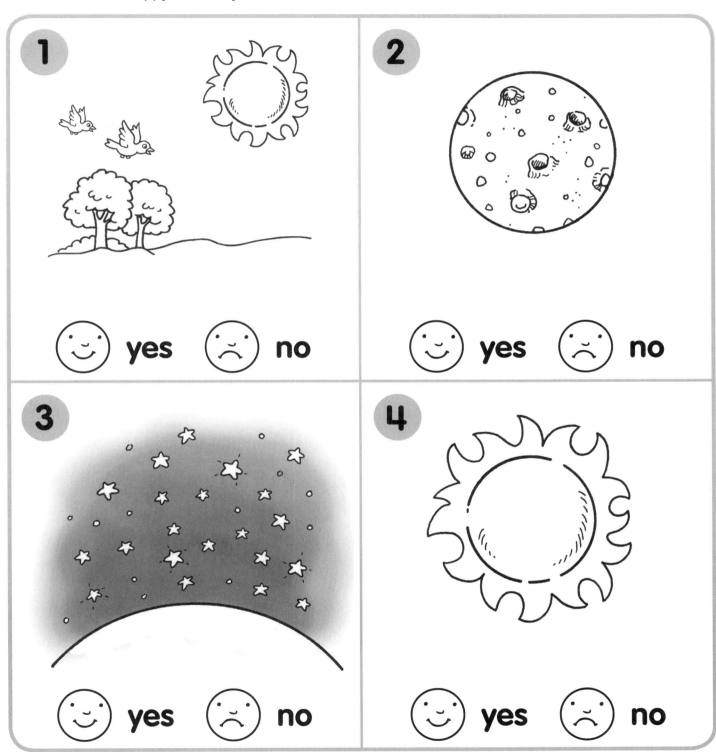

1

😊 yes   🙁 no

2

😊 yes   🙁 no

3

😊 yes   🙁 no

4

😊 yes   🙁 no

Week 17   143

What Is a Star?

Listen. Connect the stars to make the Big Dipper. Finish the picture.

Name _____

What Is a Star?

Listen and follow the directions. Trace the words and finish the sentence.

1. sun   2. star

Our sun is a star.

Name _____

What I Learned

What to Do
Have your child look at the picture below. Ask him or her to point to and name the objects in the sky. (moon, stars) Then have your child color the picture.

Science Concept: The sun, moon, and stars are objects in our sky.

To Parents
This week your child learned that a star is a giant ball of hot, glowing gas, and that stars form patterns (constellations) in the sky.

What to Do Next
Go outside with your child and observe the stars in the night sky. Then have your child draw a night scene that includes the stars.

Everyday Literacy: Science • EMC 5025 • © Evan-Moor Corp.

Bodies of Water

Science Objective:
To help students understand that Earth is mostly covered by water and that there are different bodies of water, including oceans, rivers, lakes, and ponds

Science Vocabulary:
body, globe, lake, land, ocean, pond, river, water

Day 1
SKILLS

Earth Science
• Understand that the Earth is composed of air, land, and water
• Distinguish between bodies of water

Literacy

Oral Language Development
• Respond orally to simple questions

Comprehension
• Make connections using illustrations, prior knowledge, or real-life experiences
• Answer questions about key details in a text read aloud
• Make inferences and draw conclusions

Introducing the Concept

Show students a globe and tell them it represents Earth. Say:

A globe is round like the Earth. It shows Earth's land and water. The place where we live is here (point to your location on the globe). *On this globe, what color is the land where we live?* (students respond) *What do you think the blue parts on this globe are?* (water)

> • *Most of the Earth is covered by water. There are many different types, or* **bodies**, *of water. There are oceans, rivers, lakes, and ponds.*

Listening to the Story

Distribute the Day 1 activity page to each student. Say: *Listen and look at the pictures as I read a story about a girl who has seen different bodies of water.*

My family travels to different parts of the world every summer. That's how I found out that most of the Earth is covered by water. It has oceans, rivers, lakes, and ponds. A pond is a small body of water. Horses on my uncle's farm drink from a pond. A lake is a bigger body of water, with land all around it. Last summer my family sailed a boat on a lake. Then we rode our bikes over a bridge across a river. A river is a long, narrow body of water that flows to a lake or an ocean. An ocean is the biggest body of water. Once I watched whales splash in the ocean. I wonder what bodies of water I'll see next summer!

Confirming Understanding

Distribute crayons or markers. Reinforce the science concept by asking students questions about the story. Say:

> • *Point to each body of water as I say its name:* **pond**, **lake**, **river**, **ocean**.

> • *Which one is the smallest?* (pond) *Make a dot on it. Which one is the biggest?* (ocean) *Make an* **X** *on it.*

> • *Which one flows to the ocean?* (river) *Draw a line down it. Which one did the girl go sailing on?* (lake) *Color it blue.*

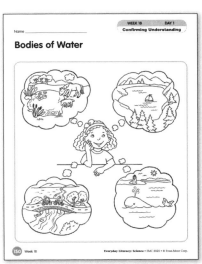

Day 1 picture

Earth Science
- Understand that the Earth is composed of air, land, and water
- Distinguish between bodies of water

Literacy

Oral Language Development
- Respond orally to simple questions

Comprehension
- Recall details
- Make connections using illustrations, prior knowledge, or real-life experiences

Reinforcing the Concept

Reread the Day 1 story. Then reinforce this week's science concept by guiding a discussion about the story. Say:

In our story, we learned that the Earth has bodies of water. What are they called? (ponds, lakes, rivers, oceans)

Distribute the Day 2 activity and crayons. Say:

- *Point to box 1. This body of water is a pond. Is a pond bigger than a lake? Color the happy face for* **yes** *or the sad face for* **no***.* (no)

- *Point to box 2. This body of water is a lake. Is a lake big enough to sail a boat on? Color the happy face for* **yes** *or the sad face for* **no***.* (yes)

- *Point to box 3. This body of water is a river. Can a river flow from a lake to an ocean? Color the happy face for* **yes** *or the sad face for* **no***.* (yes) *If you were standing on one side of a river, how could you get to the other side?* (over a bridge)

- *Point to box 4. This body of water is an ocean. Is an ocean bigger than a lake? Color the happy face for* **yes** *or the sad face for* **no***.* (yes)

Day 2 activity

Earth Science
- Understand that the Earth is composed of air, land, and water
- Distinguish between bodies of water

Literacy

Oral Language Development
- Respond orally to simple questions

Comprehension
- Make connections using illustrations, prior knowledge, or real-life experiences
- Make inferences and draw conclusions

Applying the Concept

Distribute the Day 3 activity and crayons. Then introduce the activity by reviewing:

A globe is round like the Earth. A globe shows Earth's land and water. It shows that most of the Earth is covered by bodies of water.

- *Point to the picture of the globe. The shaded areas are land. What are the other areas?* (water)

- *What color are bodies of water on a globe?* (blue) *Color the water blue.*

- *Now point to the sentence under the picture. Move your finger under the words while I read to you:* **Earth has land and water.** *Now move your finger under the words and read the sentence with me.* (students read along)

- *What is the last word in the sentence?* (water) *Trace the word* **water** *with a blue crayon.*

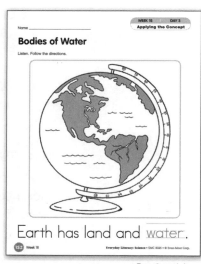

Day 3 activity

Earth Science

• Understand that the Earth is composed of air, land, and water

• Distinguish between bodies of water

Literacy

Oral Language Development

• Respond orally to simple questions

• Use new vocabulary

Comprehension

• Make connections using illustrations, prior knowledge, or real-life experiences

Applying the Concept

Review this week's science concept by inviting students to describe different bodies of water they have seen. Then distribute the Day 4 activity and crayons. Say:

The words on this page name bodies of water.

• *Put your finger on number 1. This word is* **pond**. *Move your finger under the word and read it with me:* **pond**. *What is a pond?* (smallest body of water) *Find the picture of a pond. Draw a line from the word to the picture.*

• *Put your finger on number 2. This word is* **lake**. *Read it with me:* **lake**. *What is a lake?* (bigger body of water with land all around it) *Draw a line to the lake.*

• *Put your finger on number 3. This word is* **river**. *Read it with me:* **river**. *What is a river?* (a long, flowing body of water) *Draw a line to the river.*

• *Put your finger on number 4. This word is* **ocean**. *Read it with me:* **ocean**. *What is an ocean?* (the biggest body of water) *Draw a line to the ocean.*

Day 4 activity

Earth Science

• Understand that the Earth is composed of air, land, and water

• Distinguish between bodies of water

Literacy

Oral Language Development

• Use new vocabulary

Scientific Thinking & Inquiry

• Gather and record information through simple observations and investigations

Home–School Connection p. 154
Spanish version available (see p. 2)

Hands-on Science Activity

Reinforce this week's science concept with the following hands-on activity:

Materials: sandbox or sand table, sand, shovels, containers of water

Activity: Direct students to use the sand table and water to form the bodies of water they learned about this week. Have them build small ponds, big lakes, flowing rivers, and a large ocean. Discuss their creations and encourage students to use the terms they learned for bodies of water: **pond, lake, river,** and **ocean**.

Name _____

Bodies of Water

Name _____

Bodies of Water

Listen. Color the happy face for **yes.** Color the sad face for **no.**

Name _____

Bodies of Water

Listen. Follow the directions.

Earth has land and <u>water</u>.

Name _____

Bodies of Water

Listen and read. Match the words and pictures.

1 pond •

2 lake •

3 river •

4 ocean •

Name _____

What I Learned

What to Do
Have your child look at the pictures below. Ask him or her to tell you something about each body of water. For example, *A pond is small, and animals may drink there.* Then have your child color the pictures.

Science Concept: Most of the Earth is covered by water.

To Parents
This week your child learned that most of the Earth is covered by bodies of water: ponds, lakes, rivers, and oceans.

What to Do Next
Talk about a pond, lake, river, or ocean your child has seen or visited, or plan a family trip to a nearby body of water.

Everyday Literacy: Science • EMC 5025 • © Evan-Moor Corp.

WEEK 19

Concept

Earth is composed of air, land, and water.

Looking for Rocks

Science Objective:
To help students understand that rocks, which are part of Earth's crust, can be found everywhere

Science Vocabulary:
boulder, crust, nature, pebble, rock, rough, smooth

Day 1 SKILLS

Earth Science
- Understand that the Earth is composed of air, land, and water
- Understand that rocks have different properties

Literacy

Oral Language Development
- Respond orally to simple questions

Comprehension
- Make connections using illustrations, prior knowledge, or real-life experiences
- Answer questions about key details in a text read aloud
- Make inferences and draw conclusions

Introducing the Concept

Show students a loaf of bread and cut off a slice to let them see the difference between the crust and the inside. Then say:

- *This bread has a crust. Earth has a crust, too. Most of Earth's crust is covered by water, soil, and plants. But under that, Earth's crust is rock.*
- *Where have you seen rocks?* (students respond) *Were the rocks big or small?* (all sizes) *What color were they?* (many different colors) *What shape were they?* (all different shapes)

Listening to the Story

Distribute the Day 1 activity page to each student. Say: *Listen and look at the picture as I read a story about a girl and her aunt who look for rocks.*

Yesterday, Aunt Amy and I went on a rock hunt. We saw rocks everywhere! I asked her where they came from. She said that rocks come from Earth's crust. Pieces of rock break away and wind up in all sorts of places. We found rocks along the lake. They were smooth and round from being in the water. We found rough, sharp rocks that had been cut from the hillside. Some pieces were huge and some were tiny. When I got home, I found rocks in the garden, along the path, around the flowers, and in the wall. Then I went inside and saw rocks in our kitchen! The countertop is made from a big slice of speckled rock. The floor is made from a smooth gray rock. It's fun to have pieces of Earth's crust inside my house!

Confirming Understanding

Reinforce the science concept by asking questions about the story. Ask:

- *Where did the girl find mostly smooth rocks?* (lake) *Draw a red line from the girl to the lake.*
- *Where did she find mostly rough, sharp rocks?* (hillside) *Draw a blue line from the girl to the sharp rocks.*
- *Where did she find all kinds of rocks?* (garden) *Circle three different rocks in the garden.*
- *What was made of speckled rock?* (countertop) *Draw more speckles on it.*

Day 1 picture

Day 2
SKILLS

Earth Science
- Understand that the Earth is composed of air, land, and water
- Understand that rocks have different properties

Literacy

Oral Language Development
- Name and describe pictured objects

Comprehension
- Recall details
- Make inferences and draw conclusions

Reinforcing the Concept

Reread the Day 1 story. Then reinforce this week's science concept by guiding a discussion about the story. Say:

In our story, Aunt Amy helps the girl find rocks in many places. Where did they find rocks? (lake, hillside, garden, kitchen)

Distribute the Day 2 activity and crayons. Say:

- *Point to box 1. At the lake, the girl found rocks that were smooth and round from being in the water. Do you think these rocks have been in water? Color the happy face for **yes** or the sad face for **no**.* (yes) *Why?* (They look smooth and rounded.)

- *Point to box 2. The girl saw many rocks where a bulldozer cut into a hillside. Were the rocks smooth and round? Color the happy face for **yes** or the sad face for **no**.* (no) *What did they look like?* (sharp, rough)

- *Point to box 3. It shows rocks from the garden. Did they all come from Earth's crust? Color the happy face for **yes** or the sad face for **no**.* (yes)

- *Point to box 4. What are the countertop and floor made of?* (rock) *Are they both made from the same kind of rock? Color the happy face for **yes** or the sad face for **no**.* (no) *How do you know?* (They look different.)

Day 2 activity

Day 3
SKILLS

Earth Science
- Understand that the Earth is composed of air, land, and water
- Understand that rocks have different properties

Literacy

Oral Language Development
- Use descriptive language
- Respond orally to simple questions

Comprehension
- Make connections using illustrations, prior knowledge, or real-life experiences

Applying the Concept

To introduce the activity, help students recall what they learned on Day 1. Say:

Rocks can be many sizes and shapes. Some have one color and some have many. Some feel smooth and some feel rough.

Distribute the Day 3 activity and crayons. Say:

- *Point to row 1. Rocks can be smooth or rough. How do you think the first rock in this row would feel?* (smooth) *Draw a green line under each smooth rock in this row.*

- *Point to row 2. Rocks can be big or small. What size is the first rock?* (small) *A small rock is sometimes called a **pebble**. Draw a brown line under each pebble in this row.*

- *Point to row 3. You can find rocks in many places in nature. Can you find rocks in a garden?* (yes) *Which of these other pictures show rocks in nature?* (hillside, lake) *Draw a red line under each place.*

- *Point to row 4. People use rocks to make things. Can a garden path be made of rocks?* (yes) *Which other pictures show things made of rocks?* (wall, countertop) *Draw a purple line under each thing made of rocks.*

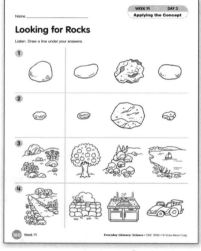

Day 3 activity

Everyday Literacy: Science • EMC 5025 • © Evan-Moor Corp.

Earth Science
- Understand that the Earth is composed of air, land, and water
- Understand that rocks have different properties

Literacy
Oral Language Development
- Name and describe pictured objects

Comprehension
- Make connections using illustrations, prior knowledge, or real-life experiences

Extending the Concept

Introduce the activity by saying:

We find different types of rocks in many places in nature. We also use rocks to make many things. Where have you seen rocks that were used to make something? (students respond)

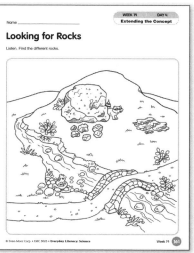

Distribute the Day 4 activity and crayons. Say:

- *Find the smooth, round rocks in the picture. Where are they?* (near/in the water) *Color two of the rocks green.*

- *Find the biggest rock in the picture. Where is it?* (on the hill) *A big rock is sometimes called a* **boulder***. Color the boulder orange.*

- *Find some rough, sharp rocks. Where are they?* (near the big rock) *Color them red.*

- *Find something that someone built out of pieces of rocks. What is it?* (a bridge) *Color the bridge brown.*

Day 4 activity

Earth Science
- Understand that the Earth is composed of air, land, and water
- Understand that rocks have different properties

Literacy

Oral Language Development
- Use descriptive language

Scientific Thinking & Inquiry
- Sort objects according to common characteristics
- Make inferences and draw conclusions

Home–School Connection p. 162
Spanish version available (see p. 2)

Hands-on Science Activity

Reinforce this week's science concept with the following hands-on activity:

Materials: rocks of different shapes, sizes, textures, and colors; table for displaying rocks

Preparation: A day or two beforehand, ask each student to bring in a rock.

Activity: Have each student show the group his or her rock and tell where it was found. Then say:

Let's sort our rocks according to where they were found. What groups can we make? (Students may suggest categories such as playground, garden, backyard, etc.)

Have each student place his or her rock in a group on the table. After discussing the various places where the rocks were found, have students sort the rocks into new groups according to color, size, texture (rough, sharp, smooth), and shape (flat, round). Encourage students to describe the characteristics of the rocks (e.g., speckled, bumpy, shiny, etc.) and to talk about how the rocks might have gotten to the places where they were found.

Looking for Rocks

Name _____

Looking for Rocks

Listen. Color the happy face for **yes**. Color the sad face for **no**.

1

yes no

2

yes no

3

yes no

4

yes no

Name _____

Looking for Rocks

Listen. Draw a line under your answers.

1

2

3

4

Name _____

Looking for Rocks

Listen. Find the different rocks.

Name _____

What I Learned

What to Do

Have your child look at the pictures below. Ask him or her to point to and name the places where the girl from the story found rocks. Talk about places where your child has seen rocks. Ask him or her to tell you about their size, shape, color, and texture (feel). Then have your child color the picture.

WEEK 19
Home–School Connection

Science Concept: Earth is composed of air, land, and water.

To Parents
This week your child learned that rocks are part of the Earth's crust and they can be found everywhere.

What to Do Next

Take a walk with your child to find rocks. Bring a small paper bag to collect some. Place them in a bucket or dishpan of water when you return home, and have your child note any changes in color.

Everyday Literacy: Science • EMC 5025 • © Evan-Moor Corp.

Concept

Water on Earth is always moving through the water cycle.

The Water Cycle

Science Objective:
To help students understand the process called the water cycle, by which water evaporates and then falls back to Earth

Science Vocabulary:
cloud, cycle, droplets, Earth, evaporate, raindrop, sun, water cycle, water vapor

Day 1
SKILLS

Earth Science
- Identify the phases of the water cycle
- Understand that land, air, and water affect the weather

Literacy

Oral Language Development
- Respond orally to simple questions
- Use new vocabulary

Comprehension
- Make connections using illustrations, prior knowledge, or real-life experiences
- Answer questions about key details in a text read aloud
- Make inferences and draw conclusions

Introducing the Concept

Begin by activating students' prior knowledge about the water cycle. Ask:

- *Where does rain come from?* (e.g., the sky, clouds)
- *After the rain falls, what does the water do?* (makes puddles, goes into the ground, flows down hills, etc.)

Explain: *There is a lot of water on Earth. When the sun warms the water, some of the water turns into tiny droplets that go into the air. It evaporates, or changes from a liquid to a gas. The droplets form clouds. The clouds grow heavy, and the water comes back down as rain. This happens over and over. When something happens over and over again, we call it a* **cycle**.

Listening to the Story

Distribute the Day 1 activity page. Say: *Listen and look at the picture as I read a story about a boy and his class who learn about the* **water cycle**.

One sunny day, Tyler and his classmates were playing outside. Suddenly, the wind began to blow. Clouds moved in. Before long, Tyler felt raindrops, and the class went inside. Tyler asked, "Where does rain come from?" Mr. Diaz explained that it comes from clouds. Clouds are made of **water vapor**, *or tiny droplets of water. When a cloud grows too heavy with vapor, the water droplets fall to Earth. That's rain! Puddles form. The sun comes out and warms Earth. The puddles disappear. The water evaporates back into the air. Then the water in the air makes new clouds! This is the* **water cycle**.

Confirming Understanding

Distribute crayons. Reinforce the science concept by asking questions about the story. Ask:

- *Where do raindrops come from?* (They fall from clouds.) *Color one of the clouds black.*
- *What happens to puddles when the sun comes out?* (They evaporate; they turn into water vapor.) *Color one puddle blue.*
- *What makes new clouds?* (water vapor) *Draw a new cloud in the sky.*

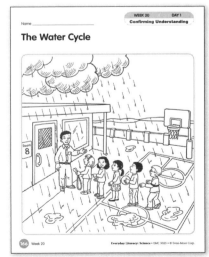

Day 1 picture

Earth Science

- Identify the phases of the water cycle
- Understand that land, air, and water affect the weather

Literacy

Oral Language Development

- Use traditional structures, such as cause and effect, to convey information
- Use new vocabulary

Comprehension

- Recall details
- Make connections using illustrations, prior knowledge, or real-life experiences

Reinforcing the Concept

Reread the Day 1 story. Then reinforce this week's science concept by discussing the story:

- *What did Tyler want to know?* (where rain came from)

- *What did Mr. Diaz tell Tyler?* (Rain comes from clouds, which are made of tiny water droplets called **water vapor**. When the clouds get heavy, rain falls.)

Distribute the Day 2 activity and crayons. Say:

- *Let's number the pictures to show how the water cycle works. First, a cloud is formed from water vapor. More and more water droplets make the cloud dark and heavy. Find the picture that shows a heavy cloud. Write **1** in the box.*

- *The cloud grows darker and heavier. What happens then?* (Water falls to Earth as rain.) *Follow the arrow that points to rain. Write **2** in the box.*

- *Next, the sun comes out and warms Earth. What happens then?* (Water evaporates into the air.) *Follow the arrow that points to the puddle evaporating in the sun. Write **3** in the box.*

- *What happens to the water that evaporates?* (It makes new clouds.) *Follow the arrow that points to the picture of a new cloud. Write **4**. Follow the last arrow. Where does it point?* (back to box 1, the heavy cloud)

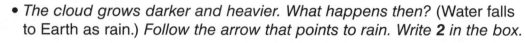

Day 2 activity

Earth Science

- Identify the phases of the water cycle
- Understand that land, air, and water affect the weather

Literacy

Oral Language Development

- Use traditional structures, such as cause and effect, to convey information

Comprehension

- Make connections using illustrations, prior knowledge, or real-life experiences
- Make inferences and draw conclusions

Applying the Concept

Distribute the Day 3 activity and crayons. Then introduce the activity by reviewing:

*Water evaporates and makes clouds. Then the water falls back to Earth as rain. This process is called the **water cycle**.*

- *Point to the first picture. What do you see?* (a cloud) *What will happen after the cloud grows heavy?* (It will rain.) *Draw a line to the picture of rain coming from the cloud.*

- *Point to picture 2. What is the boy doing?* (playing outdoors) *It's starting to rain. What will he probably do next?* (go inside) *Draw a line to the picture of him playing indoors.*

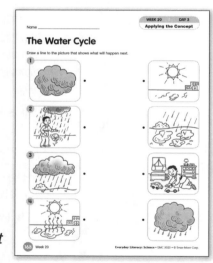

Day 3 activity

- *Point to picture 3. What do you see?* (a lot of rain pouring down from cloud) *What will the rain make on the ground?* (puddles) *Draw a line to the picture that shows rain puddles.*

- *Point to picture 4. What is happening?* (The warm sun is shining on the puddle.) *What will happen to the puddle?* (It will get smaller and disappear.) *Draw a line to the picture that shows the puddle drying up.*

Day 4
SKILLS

Earth Science
- Identify the phases of the water cycle
- Understand that land, air, and water affect the weather

Literacy

Oral Language Development
- Use traditional structures, such as cause and effect, to convey information

Comprehension
- Make connections using illustrations, prior knowledge, or real-life experiences
- Make inferences and draw conclusions

Applying the Concept

Distribute the Day 4 activity and crayons. Then introduce the activity by saying:

Earth's water is used again and again in the water cycle. What things are part of the water cycle? (water, clouds, rain, sun, air)

- *Point to number 1. This word is **cloud**. Let's read it: **cloud**. How do clouds form?* (from water droplets in the air) *Trace the word **cloud**.*

- *Point to number 2. This word is **rain**. Let's read it: **rain**. When does rain fall from a cloud?* (when the cloud has gotten too heavy with water droplets) *Trace the word **rain**.*

- *Point to number 3. This word is **sun**. Read it with me: **sun**. What happens when the sun warms the water in a puddle?* (The water evaporates into the air.) *Trace the word **sun**.*

- *Look at number 4. This word is the same as the first word on the page. What is it?* (cloud) *When water evaporates into the air, it makes a new cloud. Trace the word **cloud**. Then draw a new cloud in the box.*

- *Now let's read all the words together: **cloud, rain, sun, cloud**.*

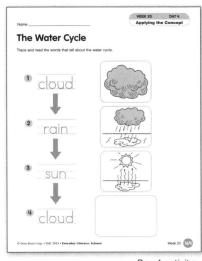

Day 4 activity

Day 5
SKILLS

Earth Science
- Identify the phases of the water cycle
- Understand that land, air, and water affect the weather

Literacy

Oral Language Development
- Use traditional structures, such as cause and effect, to convey information

Scientific Thinking & Inquiry
- Make inferences and draw conclusions
- Gather and record information through simple observations and investigations

Home–School Connection p. 170
Spanish version available (see p. 2)

Hands-on Science Activity

Reinforce this week's science concept with the following hands-on activity:

Materials: two identical socks per student (have each student bring in a pair), water

Activity: On a sunny day, have students help or observe you as you thoroughly wet the socks. Say:

- *The sun is an important part of the water cycle because it warms the water. What does the sun do to a puddle?* (dries it up; makes the water evaporate)

- *We are going to show how the sun's warmth makes water evaporate.*

Have students place one sock outside to dry in the sunlight and the other in the shade. Allow students to check the socks periodically and observe which ones dry first. Then ask:

- *Why did the socks in the sun dry first?* (because the sun warmed the water in the socks and made it evaporate)

Name _____

The Water Cycle

Everyday Literacy: Science • EMC 5025 • © Evan-Moor Corp.

Name _____

The Water Cycle

Listen. Follow the arrows with your finger. Then write a number in each box.

The Water Cycle

Draw a line to the picture that shows what will happen next.

1

2

3

4

Everyday Literacy: Science • EMC 5025 • © Evan-Moor Corp.

The Water Cycle

Trace and read the words that tell about the water cycle.

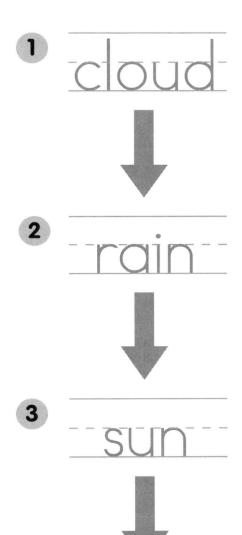

1. cloud

2. rain

3. sun

4. cloud

Name _____

What I Learned

What to Do

The picture shows the water cycle. Have your child describe what is happening at each phase. (1. Clouds made of tiny water droplets get heavy. 2. Water falls to Earth as rain. 3. The sun warms Earth. The water evaporates into the air. 4. The water in the air makes new clouds.)

WEEK 20

Home–School Connection

Science Concept: Water on Earth is always moving through the water cycle.

To Parents
This week your child learned that Earth's water is recycled in a process called the water cycle.

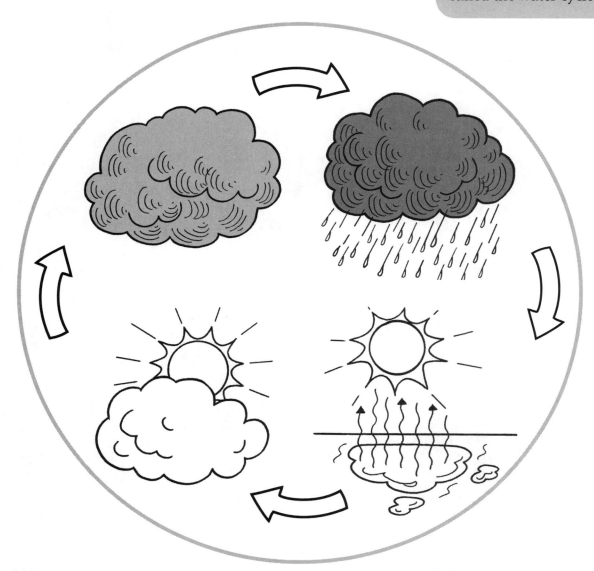

What to Do Next

Do a science experiment together with your child. Place enough water in each of two pie tins to cover the bottom. Put one in the sun and the other in the shade. Check them periodically to see which one evaporates first. (The sun warms the water in one pan and it evaporates first.)

Answer Key

Week 1

Day 1

Day 2

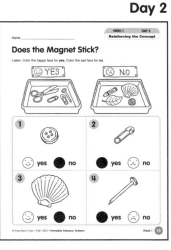

Day 3

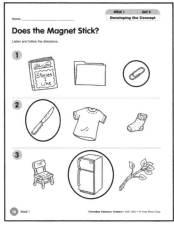

Day 4

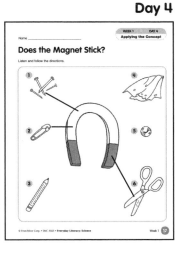

Week 2

Day 1

Day 2

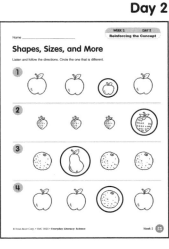

Day 3

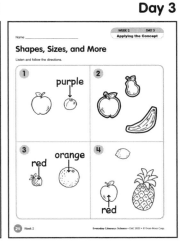

Day 4

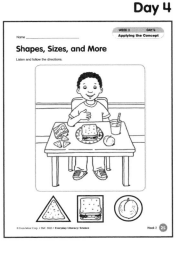

Week 3

Day 1

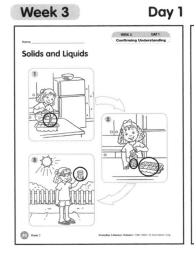

Day 2

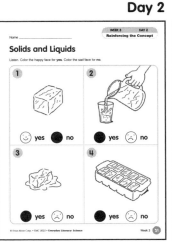

Day 3

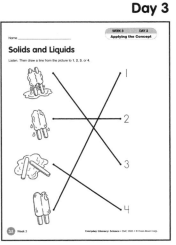

Day 4

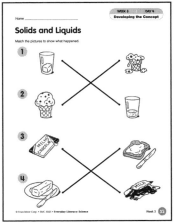

Week 4

| Day 1 | Day 2 | Day 3 | Day 4 |

Where Did the Water Go?

Answers will vary.

Where Did the Water Go?

Listen. Then draw a line from the picture to 1, 2, or 3.

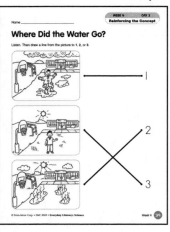

Where Did the Water Go?

Listen and follow the directions. Draw lines to match.

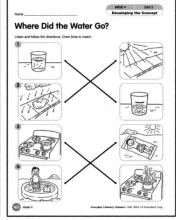

Where Did the Water Go?

Listen. Then draw a line from the picture to 1, 2, 3, or 4.

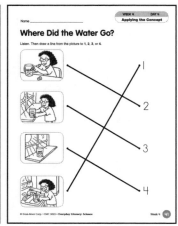

Week 5

| Day 1 | Day 2 | Day 3 | Day 4 |

Wheels Do the Work

green
brown
red
Color one wheel black.

Wheels Do the Work

Listen. Color the happy face for **yes**. Color the sad face for **no**.

Wheels Do the Work

Circle the people who are using wheels to make their work easier.

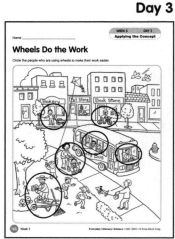

Wheels Do the Work

Draw a line to match.

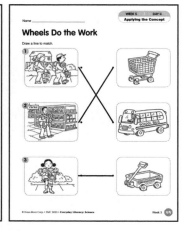

Week 6

| Day 1 | Day 2 | Day 3 | Day 4 |

Tell Where It Is
Answers will vary, but only one toy should have a red dot.

brown
green
A toy should be drawn.

Tell Where It Is

Listen. Color the happy face for **yes**. Color the sad face for **no**.

Tell Where It Is

Listen and follow the directions.

| on | in | next to | below | above |

Answers will vary, but only one bird should be colored yellow.

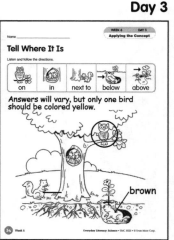

brown

Tell Where It Is

Listen and follow the directions.

Drawings will vary.

Everyday Literacy: Science • EMC 5025 • © Evan-Moor Corp.

Week 7	**Day 1**	**Day 2**	**Day 3**	**Day 4**

Week 8	**Day 1**	**Day 2**	**Day 3**	**Day 4**

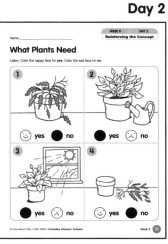

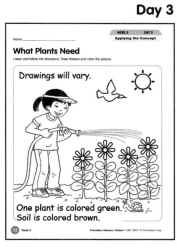

Week 9	**Day 1**	**Day 2**	**Day 3**	**Day 4**

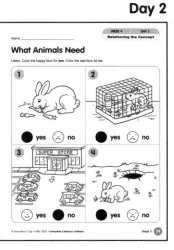

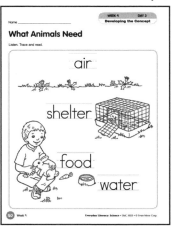

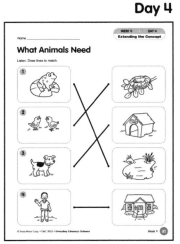

Week 10	Day 1	Day 2	Day 3	Day 4

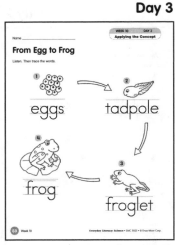
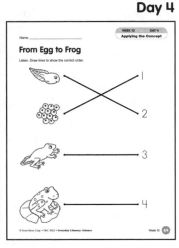

Week 11	Day 1	Day 2	Day 3	Day 4

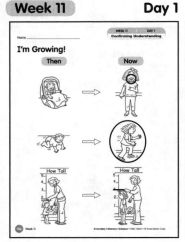

Week 12	Day 1	Day 2	Day 3	Day 4

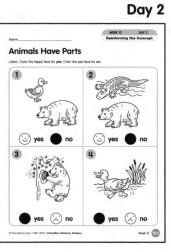
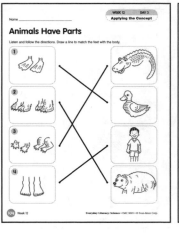
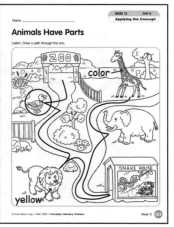

Week 13

Day 1

Day 2

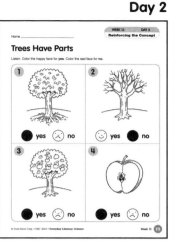

Day 3

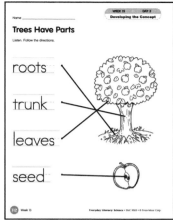

Day 4

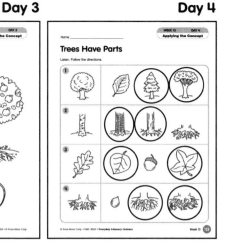

Week 14

Day 1

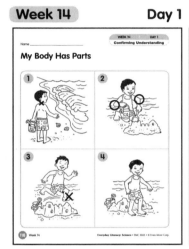

Day 2

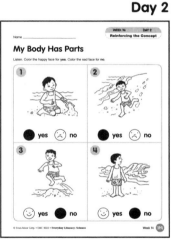

Day 3

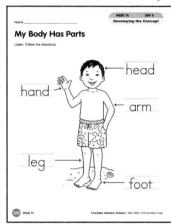

Day 4

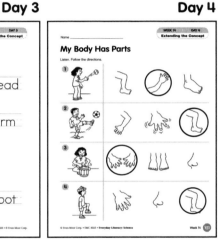

Week 15

Day 1

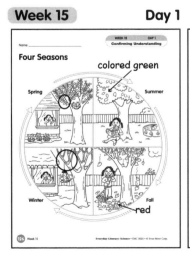

Day 2

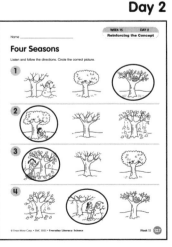

Day 3

Day 4

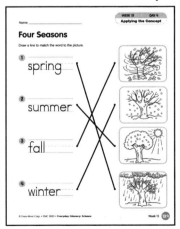

Week 16	Day 1	Day 2	Day 3	Day 4

Week 16

Day 1 — The Moon

Day 2 — The Moon

Day 3 — The Moon

Day 4 — The Moon
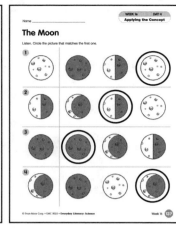

Week 17

Day 1 — What Is a Star?
Answers will vary.
yellow

Day 2 — What Is a Star?
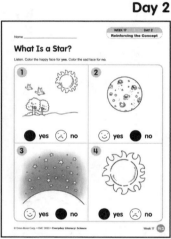

Day 3 — What Is a Star?
Drawings will vary.
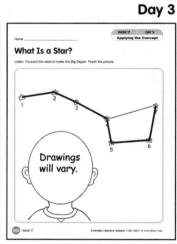

Day 4 — What Is a Star?
Should be colored.
1. sun   2. star
Our sun is a star.

Week 18

Day 1 — Bodies of Water
blue

Day 2 — Bodies of Water
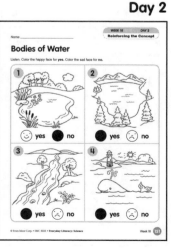

Day 3 — Bodies of Water
blue
blue
Earth has land and water.
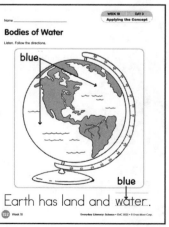

Day 4 — Bodies of Water
1 pond
2 lake
3 river
4 ocean
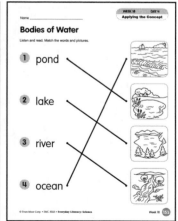